The Student Journalist
and
INTERVIEWING

Rappelling, backpacking, canoeing, water skiing—many a student struggles through the "scholarly" pursuits dictated by the classroom with visions of the weekend activities in mind—and many a reporter sees story possibilities in the colorful outdoor sports young people enjoy.

THE
STUDENT
JOURNALIST
GUIDE
SERIES

THE STUDENT JOURNALIST AND
INTERVIEWING

by

HAZEL PRESSON

PUBLISHED BY
RICHARDS ROSEN
PRESS, INC.
NEW YORK

Published in 1967, 1979 by Richards Rosen Press, Inc.

Copyright 1967, 1979 by Hazel Presson

Library of Congress Cataloging in Publication Data

Presson, Hazel.
   Interviewing.

   (The Student journalist guide series)
   First ed. published in 1967 under title: The student journalist and interviewing.
   Bibliography: p.
   SUMMARY: Offers advice on how to prepare for and conduct an interview and how to turn the raw material into a story.
   1. Interviewing (Journalism) 2. College and school journalism. [1. Interviewing (Journalism) 2. Journalism] I. Title.
PN4784.I6P7   1978   070.4′3   78–21266

ISBN 0–8239–0488–1

Revised Edition 1979

ABOUT THE AUTHOR

Hazel Presson is a combination adviser-teacher-author whose experience with high school newspapers dates back to a sunny spring morning when the editor of the school paper dashed into a freshman English class in search of someone who could read proof in an emergency.

"That was a much more important day than it seemed at the time," she observes. "The teacher recommended me—and I've been associated with school publications ever since."

That association has led to a wide experience with scholastic publications and organizations, including teaching journalism at Westark Community College and Northside High School in Fort Smith, Arkansas, both the yearbook and newspaper there holding top ratings from national scholastic press associations and in state and regional competition.

"We never have a dull moment," she says, "for in newspaper work you wake up every day in a new world. It's exciting to know what's going on—and fun to pass the news on to others."

A member of Phi Beta Kappa, Miss Presson holds an M.A. degree from the University of Arkansas and has done additional work in journalism at the University of Oklahoma as a Newspaper Fund Fellow, at Columbia University under a grant from *Life* magazine, and at the University of Minnesota as recipient of a Jostens Award. Among honors she holds are the Gold Key and the Golden Crown from the Columbia Scholastic Press Association, the Pioneer Award from the National Scholastic Press Association, and the Golden Quill from the University of Texas. She is a past president of the Columbia Scholastic Press Advisers Association.

In addition to serving as a judge and consultant in the critical services, Miss Presson participates in conferences, workshops, and short courses.

About the Author

"Whether it's a half-day drive-in sponsored by a small high school or two weeks on a university campus, it's exciting to see young people interested in producing newspapers, yearbooks, and magazines," she says. "Every staff has a special situation—and yet most of us face the same problems and needs. I've had the same questions asked from New York to Mexican Hat and from Chicago to Pickles Gap."

After school hours the adviser-teacher becomes the author, being presently engaged on a book of short stories, following a light contemporary novel and a historical novel that grew out of research for *The Story of Arkansas,* a history adopted as a state text. In addition to this volume on interviewing, she is the author of two other books in this series, *The Student Journalist and News Reporting* and *The Student Journalist and Layout,* published by the Richards Rosen Press.

CONTENTS

Preface   9

Part One: Interviewing Is of Basic Importance

    I. Definitions First   11
    II. What This Means to the Journalist   16
    III. Kinds of Interview Stories   23
    IV. Starting Point for Beginners   32

Part Two: Preparing for the Interview

    V. Understanding Your Assignment   37
    VI. Working Out a Story Line   45
    VII. Seeking Background Information   50
    VIII. Planning Questions   58
    IX. What You Should Know about People   62

Part Three: Conducting the Interview

    X. The Opening Moments   69
    XI. Keeping the Interviewee Talking   76
    XII. Watching for New Angles   80
    XIII. Noting Added Details of Setting, Personality   84
    XIV. Summary Checklist   89
    XV. Taking Notes   93

Part Four: Writing the Story

    XVI. Study Your Notes, Seek Fresh Approach   97
    XVII. Summarize Your Information   102
    XVIII. Organize and Outline   106
    XIX. Work Out a Lead   111
    XX. Follow with the Body of the Story   125

Contents

Part Five: Developing Skills in Effective Expression

XXI.	Writing Is Both an Art and a Craft	135
XXII.	A Do-It-Yourself Program	140
XXIII.	Revise, Revise, Revise	146

Part Six: A Word from the Professional Journalist — 151

Part Seven: Suggestions from Student Editors — 163

For Further Reading — 180

Acknowledgments — 184

PREFACE

"Now," said the speaker, "are there any questions that you student editors would like to ask?"

It was one of those meetings where the young and old, experienced and inexperienced, gather to exchange ideas and techniques and hope for moral support.

A serious-faced girl raised her hand.

"I think I have two problems," she said. "I'm just newly appointed an editor for next year. I'm afraid I won't know what questions to ask—or what to do with the information when I get it."

A murmur of laughter rippled across the room. "That's right," someone added from the back row. "I've worked on our paper two years, and I know—that's our number one problem."

If we consider this thoughtfully, we decide that her problem is *our* problem, our number one problem.

And so that is where this book begins. It is a new book about a very old subject.

It is new, because, as far as I know, there is no single volume like it available anywhere.

It is old, because even in the dawn of time, people discovered an interest in one another. From then on, there have been questions asked and answers given:

What is your name? What are you doing? Will you show me too? What happened? Where? When? What does it mean? Will it happen again? Et cetera, as the King of Siam would say, et cetera, et cetera, et cetera.

In most instances, of course, this is for mere personal satisfaction. But as the ages have rolled along, this information has become the body of our writing.

Meeting people. Asking questions. Seems very simple, doesn't it? That is, until you begin to think about getting started.

And suddenly you are about as self-confident as you would be on the first day of a safari in lion country.

Well, you aren't on a safari like that, and your lions may be only the principal and the deans and the teachers and your classmates. But as you would need a guide on a safari, you need a guidebook here.

Fortunately, if you can read, you can get help. In this volume are numbers of ideas and suggestions from professional journalists and teachers. With these, are numerous examples taken from school papers which have earned top ratings in national, regional and state critical services.

All this, of course, is directed to the beginner, for this series is intended for the student and the adviser who have had no training yet and no experience.

But whether inexperienced or experienced, we who are members of newspaper staffs and we who are advisers encounter much the same problems every day—same deadlines, same sad morning when we awake with no idea within a mile (and the resulting dismal feeling that we are not only bores but complete failures) —same uncooperative people to deal with, same dull world.

This book opens on a note of optimism. *You can help yourself.* You *can* solve your problems. You *can* learn how to ask the right questions and get the right answers—and then know what to do with them.

You *can* find the guides to a better and happier way of doing things.

So here's to you . . .

HAZEL PRESSON

PART ONE

Interviewing Is of Basic Importance

Chapter I

DEFINITIONS FIRST

Questions.
Answers.
Two phases of a process as old as the language of communication.
Asking the right questions and *getting the right answers*—two phases of communication as contemporary as today's news story.
This slender volume is designed to be a help to everyone who wants to know more about how to obtain the information he seeks. It is a summary of the methods and techniques of master journalists and master teachers. It includes psychological principles and philosophy.
It is a kind of how-to-do-it-yourself manual to enable you to bridge a span of inexperience so you can achieve maximum results in a comparatively short time.
It is designed especially for student journalists just beginning to work on school publications, and for inexperienced advisers who find themselves confronted with the necessity of helping an untrained staff produce a school paper worthy of their efforts.
Asking questions and getting answers implies a personal relationship. The word we use for this is *interview*. We borrowed it from the French, who spell it *entrevue*. That, in turn, comes

from an older expression of theirs, *s'entrevoir,* translated to mean *to visit with each other.*

Since most interviews are conducted in person, it seems that whatever would make one a more pleasant companion would have some bearing here.

A Matter of Personality

In personality studies, it has been estimated that a person's personality shortcomings defeat him many times more often than his lack of special ability does.

Suggestion: Study to improve your personality and learn as much as possible of what is called "acceptable social manners."

To paraphrase: "The career you save may be your own."

The word interview is used as both a noun and a verb. As a noun, it has three meanings: (1) a formal meeting for consultation; a conference; as, an interview with the president; (2) a meeting between a representative of the press and the person interviewed, at which the former elicits by questioning, or the latter volunteers, information for publication; (3) the statement so obtained.

As a verb, the word interview means (1) to have an interview with; (2) to question or converse with, especially in order to obtain information for publication.

Age of the Quickie

This is the Age of the Quickie. Instant coffee . . . instant headache relief . . . instant breakfast . . .

But there is no instant interview success.

Proficiency comes only with practice. In fact, it comes only with studied practice, for repetition alone does not spell success.

To succeed, you must understand the philosophy of interviewing and the psychology of human behavior—then diligently study the principles and techniques that have been found successful.

Obviously, then, you must try to put into practice these understandings and this study. Through practice you must gain experience.

This experience has been defined in various ways—depending on the point of view. Whatever the definition, however, the basic principle is the same: finding out how to do the job better and more quickly—in comparison with other persons, or in comparison with your own previous efforts.

("Experience," says the humorist Franklin P. Jones, "is what you get from being inexperienced. It's what causes you to make new mistakes instead of the same old ones.")

Few persons can afford the luxury nowadays of devoting long periods of time to getting experience the hard way—by personal trial and error.

To the journalist, certainly, it is important to have any kind of quick help possible, for no one moves at a faster pace in today's world than the journalist does—even the inexperienced journalist on a school paper.

First Things First

To develop skill in interviewing is to develop the basis for successful news reporting. In fact, it is to develop the basis for any kind of writing the journalist may want to do. For stories are based on action—and action involves people.

The *what* and the *who* are the two most important of the Five W's—what, who, when, where, why.

Actually, the *who* is the most important of the five, for though the reader may ask "What happened?" or "What's going on?" he generally is interested in these answers as they concern people.

As the journalist gives the answers to these questions, he really is telling about people, for he finds the answers by asking the people who were involved in the action.

The successful journalist is one who (1) can decide just which persons to interview, (2) can set up the interview to his advantage, (3) can ask the questions the reader would ask if he were there, (4) can detect any other interesting items that the reader would like to know about, (5) can write the story in clear, concise language so the reader can understand easily, (6) can view the subject with an enthusiasm that shows through the words he writes, so the reader has a vivid, colorful account, (7) can understand the significance of the event and possible relationships, and interpret these correctly so the reader knows what the story means to him.

No Secret Formula

Professional writers are frequently asked, "What is your formula, your secret of success?"

This sometimes can be difficult for them, as in the case of

An experienced journalism student can often help a beginner by checking copy with him. However, both must understand the delicate relationship between a writer (even a beginner) and anyone who would want to be a helpful teacher and critic. Before you ask for criticism, be sure that you are seeking help, not praise. To the critic: Be considerate. Adverse comment can hurt.

Jim G. Lucas when he was covering the action in Korea for the Scripps-Howard Newspaper Alliance, Washington, D.C. His editors decided that since he had been on the job so long in such a rigorous campaign, it would be a help to send another correspondent to assist him. In notifying Lucas about this, they cabled: "Give him the formula."

"That stumped me," Lucas said. "I didn't know, still don't know. I don't even know if I have one. I began writing, and it started clicking. Don't ask me how or why."

True, there are no magic formulas here.

However, what professional writers often overlook is that in the long period of training, there are many procedures, many suggestions, many techniques that serve well from one situation to another. It is these that help the beginner.

And a Matter of Caring

Success will come only if you want to succeed. For here, as in so many other areas, the secret lies in *caring*. If you *care* enough to try, then success can be yours.

Success, like happiness, never comes wrapped up neatly in packages that you can order when you please. Like happiness, success is more *a way of traveling* than an end result.

Chapter II

WHAT THIS MEANS TO THE JOURNALIST

Interviewing can hardly be discussed without immediate and constant reference to reporting the news, for the two are closely related.

In fact, almost all news and feature stories—for newspapers, magazines, radio, and television—are based on material gained through interviews.

The head of the public relations department at the University of Oklahoma asserts that, according to his estimate, interviewing is basic to nine of every ten stories a journalist does.

What Is News?

Every reporter is looking for material for stories, interesting stories that will appeal to his readers. When he has a story idea, he then seeks the best person or persons to interview.

In choosing subjects, he considers the old familiar elements of news evaluation.

That is, he asks himself these questions:

(1) Is this story interesting to readers because . . . it is timely?

(2) . . . it has names of well-known people, or people familiar to the reader?

(3) . . . it is in the reader's locality?

(4) . . . it is important to the well-being of the reader?

(5) . . . it contains some element of drama?

(6) . . . it is unusual?

(7) . . . it is humorous?

(8) . . . it has some quality of human interest?

Frequently these questions are stated another way. The writer looks for stories that "run the N line":

(1) newness, (2) nearness, (3) nowness—and, of course, always (4) names.

The professional journalist always has his ear tuned for any word suggesting a story that answers one or more of these questions.

He "thinks journalism" all the time, as William Jay Stewart, of the *Oklahoma Journal,* puts it.

To Test Your Idea

Is there a way you can test the news value of an idea you may have for a story?

Yes, says R. M. Neal in his book *News Gathering and News Writing.*

Try to decide the extent to which the readers will identify themselves with the story, he says. Go over these items for each story idea:

(1) Is this an event which the readers watched, though they did not take part?

(2) Is this a happening in which the reader shared or participated? or would like to share or participate?

(3) Is this news concerning a well-known person or place?

(4) Is this news of a field parallel to one in which the readers themselves are interested?

(5) Is this a name gleaming with mystery, romance, intrigue, etc.?

(6) News that interprets or clarifies a little understood action?

(7) News of "automatic" interest because it stirs or appeals to some trait or concern found in so many readers as to be "general" or even "universal"? (For example: conflict, struggle, fights, competition, sympathy, children, romance, sex, mystery.)

News Without Events

"News without events" may seem like a strange phrase to you if you are just beginning to get an idea of what journalism is today. But it is generally understood among journalists that the notion that "something must happen" is an out-of-date conception of the news story.

News, they say, lies also in trends, situations, conditions, interpretations. Whatever people are talking about today—or will be talking about tomorrow—is news.

Interpretive Reporting

In this brief summary of news values, a word should be added about interpretive reporting.

Today there is increasing emphasis on reporting in depth. That is, the reporter tries to present the news so the reader understands more about it. The *why* and the *how* of the story are given as fully as possible.

"Depth reporting adds a personality to the *who,* a definition to the *what,* a dimension to the *when,* a location to the *where,* a cause to the *why,* and a reason to the *how.*"

That's how Paul S. Swensson of the Newspaper Fund, Inc. defines it. He goes on to say:

"The depth reporter's task, beyond writing a clear, interesting story, is to make sure that he has not omitted any information which is significant to understanding, nor confused the reader with unnecessary facts.

"The depth report gives the reader more than just facts. It helps him understand what is behind the news. It relates current events to the past and projects them into the future.

"Thus, the reporter does not simply say that the history-making Beatles were a tremendously successful group making a lot of money. He would ask teen-agers, parents, teachers, musicians, song publishers, disc jockeys, psychologists, and sociologists why they thought the Liverpool lads were so popular. Their replies, their opinions, their theories would add dimension to the story. In doing all this, the reporter is balancing facts and opinions about his subject, placing them in perspective for the reader, so he understands more fully.

"How close can a school newspaper come to depth reporting? Perhaps one or two stories a year in the hands of a top student, or students. Even then the student would be restricted to some degree in gathering his information, but if the topic were carefully chosen, he could overcome this obstacle. For example, a form of depth reporting could be used on school government stories; on the need for expansion of the school's physical plant; on local student driving safety; on the growth of a local student

In all kinds of reporting, pictures are important in developing the story and in gaining interest. This is especially true in interpretive reporting, for every help is needed to give the reader a better understanding.

fad; how students spend their money or time; or scholarships and the selection of a college."

Perspective Meaning

Another way of saying this is that the task of reporters today is providing not only the events of the news, but also the *background, depth, perspective, and meaning* for the news.

We might explain the idea this way:

The actual account of the news event is a kind of *news bulletin*. What we call a *news story* is the account of the event *plus* the added values that the capable reporter can gather and impart when he has an opportunity to dig more deeply.

This continuity and perspective are necessary—or the reader becomes hopelessly bogged down in the details of contemporary history.

"The news has become definitely complex," says Lester Markel, of the *New York Times*. "Think of the huge and pressing questions that have descended upon us! What single mind can comprehend half the issues that confront us on a single day? Newspapers must aim more at understanding than ever before."

The whys and hows of the event are as important as the event itself, says Emanuel Freedman, of the *New York Times*. "We want our correspondents to spot trends and to anticipate the event. The event itself sometimes serves merely as a take-off point for a wrap-up of trends."

A different wording of the same idea is voiced by the *Time-Life* publications. "What we want to know are the reasons something happened," says Richard M. Clurman, chief of correspondents for *Time-Life*. "To the correspondent this is a hellishly difficult but enormously stimulating assignment."

Erwin D. Canham, of the *Christian Science Monitor,* says, "A *Monitor* correspondent handles news as quickly as possible but seeks as soon as he can to give his copy as much perspective as it is in his power to do."

Another way of explaining this is found in the kind of advertising put out by the various broadcasting companies. The National Broadcasting Company, for example, in speaking of the Chancellor-Brinkley report says:

"To report the news and its significance fully and fairly—not merely so that it be understood, but so that it cannot be *mis*understood . . . to convey to the viewer more information, a greater depth of analysis, and a keener sense of the world around him. As one viewer put it, 'I just feel that when I watch Chancellor and Brinkley, I've got a better idea of what's going on.' "

All of which makes this point: that merely a mass of facts does not constitute a news story. The able reporter, with perceptiveness and skill in interviewing the sources from whom he gets his facts, supplies the difference.

To summarize: Reporting is not merely saying, "Here are the facts." The reporter's purpose is to discover what the facts mean to the reader.

Why Interpretation?

The reason for this focusing on interpretive reporting is summarized in a book entitled *Commitment to Freedom* by Erwin D. Canham.

"Newspapers must give people the tools to work out their salvation," he asserts, "for mankind needs to reawaken from the false dream of security in materialism.

"The tools they need are (1) information—people need to be told the facts as clearly and as closely as possible; (2) explanation of the information—the paper must dig into the news, give perspective to events—relate today to yesterday and tomorrow; (3) the arousing of dormant thinking.

"To understand the news gives the citizen the means of action . . . to protect, preserve and advance the values and opportunities which make up what we call the free way of life."

Interview as Background

In delving into the significance of the news and its interpretation for the reader, many professional journalists underscore the importance of interviewing skill.

Anne O'Hare McCormick, of the *New York Times,* speaks for many others when she says that she considers interviews valuable as background.

"The head of a government is not likely to reveal in an interview anything he would not say in a public speech," she says. "But he does reveal himself—and this is of the utmost importance to the interpretation of the action in which his character, his vanities and ambition, his personal reactions are decisive factors."

Definition of a Reporter

With purposes of such scope, what then is the person we call a reporter? What kind of individual must he be if he expects to succeed?

In an article entitled "Good-bye to the Scoop Artist in a Trench Coat," John M. Hightower, of the Associated Press, defines a reporter today as not only a communicator of facts but also as an organizer and processor of the facts to make them interesting and understandable to the reader.

For this reason, he must have a good general education, abundant enthusiasm, and the widest possible base of general intelligence.

He should understand the technique of his art and should be able to bring to any assignment a massive curiosity about what he does not know.

"His greatest asset," Hightower says, "is his ability to view men and their affairs with detachment and to report fairly what he sees—and if possible with zest and humor."

To the beginner this may sound overwhelming. But take heart. No one ever said journalism was an easy way to anything.

What *is* in store for those who choose to be student journalists is an introduction to a whole new way of looking at the world— for you meet so many interesting people and discover so many interesting ideas.

And a whole new way of looking at yourself, and at your place in the Great Scheme of Things.

Chapter III

KINDS OF INTERVIEW STORIES

Howard Johnson has his 28 Flavors, Heinz has his 57 Varieties, and the journalist may well have his 99 Possibilities.

Why? Because with skill in interviewing, the journalist's range is bounded only by his horizons.

This applies to all—students or professionals.

As you begin to write stories for your school paper—and as you begin to read the newspapers with a better understanding—you will note that you can divide into three groups those stories in which interviewing plays an important part.

First, you can see how much of the information printed is gained from the reporter's asking questions of someone and getting answers. In this kind of story, the subject itself is of primary interest.

For example: the story about the senior play, the student council convention, the new courses to be offered next year.

Although the facts were gained from a person or persons whom the reporter selected as the source of information, only the interviewee's name is mentioned, plus identification, so the reader will know that the interviewee speaks with authority on the subject.

Second, you will note that in many stories the interviewee figures as a person. That is, the story is about the interviewee himself.

For example: the student council president's role as convention delegate, the cadet teacher's first day with her first class, a "personality story" about the winner of the oratorical contest, a story about the rodeo clown who visited the campus for a benefit show.

In each of these, the person himself is of major interest. The reader knows about him as a colorful individual who has had some part in interesting action.

Third, occasionally you find stories in which the question asked is of more importance than either the news event (as in the first group) or the person (as in the second).

For example: What do students think about the new regulation that no one will be granted a diploma who has less than a 1.5 grade average? What do students think about the effectiveness of team teaching? What do students consider the most important extracurricular activities?

Straight News

Most of us use the term "straight news" to indicate the type of story mentioned above as the first kind gained by interviewing. However, several other kinds of story fall into this grouping.

The point here is that the material of the story has to do with a subject rather than with a person. This subject may be an event, a situation, a trend, or the like—and the story itself may be what we call a feature news story rather than a straight news story. (A feature news story is one in which some element of special interest is played up.)

Even editorials (giving the writer's opinion on a subject) are often not composed until after the writer has had opportunity to interview one or more persons on the matter.

In many of these stories, the information is gained by interviewing only one person. For example:

For a story about the enrollment in your school, you probably would find the answers to all your questions by visiting only the registrar, for enrollment is in his department.

For a story about the new landscaping, you would probably visit the building and grounds engineer, who is expected to know about what is going on in his department.

If the Future Teachers plan to visit an elementary school next week, you can probably find all the information you need by interviewing the FTA president.

Caution: If you depend on *one* person for your information, be *sure* that you select the authority who knows the RIGHT answers. Also, have it understood that in the event of a change in plans, he will let you know.

Need you be warned that there are those who speak in loud voices as they utter incorrect sentences? They give the impression of "knowing all" as they speak boldly.

No one can protect you from these but yourself. Your only defense is in choosing your source of information after careful deliberation—and then in checking, checking, checking.

A True Story

Many student editors have faced the problem that was being discussed at a workshop. One editor said:

"Our student council president has been angry about a story we ran. He had agreed to give us the facts—and then at the time of the interview left the vice-president in charge, saying that he had another appointment.

"Mistake #1—Our reporter took the story without checking to see that the vice-president was fully informed.

"Mistake #2—He took 'second-hand quotes' from both the president and the sponsor.

"Mistake #3—He failed to check both the 'quotes' and the 'facts' with the president and the sponsor.

"That incorrect story created a crisis, as everyone blamed us for the errors. What was intended to be an informational and interpretive story ended by damaging our image."

Several Sources

Many times, however, no one person can supply all the answers you seek. Therefore, you must go to others.

Again, as in choosing the one source to interview, it is imperative that you consider carefully in order to select the authoritative sources. Here, in interviewing a group, you have an additional problem:

Be *sure* that you find all the sources of information so you can construct a complete story. For example, to interview only three teachers about the club carnival is to get an incomplete story if five clubs are involved in the activity.

To summarize: Your purpose is to find information—all the information to make your story complete. That is, all the answers to the questions your readers would want you to ask.

Sidebar Ideas

Since the purpose of this kind of interview is to gain facts about some subject in relation to which the interviewee is not important, you do not include the personality, conduct, and background of the interviewee in your writing. (You do, of course, identify him, so the reader will know why you chose him as the authority for your questions.)

But note: If, as you conduct the interview, you see something that interests you about the interviewee—or about something he mentions—file this away in your mind (or better, jot it down in your notes) and return to it later for another story, perhaps a feature.

This kind of "creative listening" can lead to many unexpected experiences. And in the journalist's world, an interesting experience means a possible story. The professional journalist uses the word "tips" in speaking of these possible ideas for stories.

Tips, of course, don't come from interviews alone—for the journalist who is enthusiastic about his work is always aware—and a mind alert is bound to gather in tips of many kinds.

The tip frequently turns into a better story than the original assignment.

Why? Because the writer goes into it with his whole enthusiasm.

And, in writing, enthusiasm is one way to spell success.

Person Is Important

In many stories where the information is gained from interviewing, the interviewee figures as a person. These stories are often called "interviews," perhaps to distinguish them.

The word "interview," however, is also used to refer to the

third kind of story mentioned above, the interview where the question asked is of basic interest.

These interviews in which the interviewee figures as a person fall into four groups:

(1) You interview a well-known person on a subject about which he is an expert or on which he can speak with authority.

For example: Your senator discusses with you the role of young people in political rallies in the forthcoming campaign. The head coach discusses with you careers in athletics. A local doctor expresses himself on the subject of sleeping pills and tranquilizers.

(2) You interview a well-known person on some timely subject, where what he thinks might be of interest or value to the reader.

For example:

"What can this student body do to improve the teen-age image in this community?" You discuss this with the president of the student body.

Or, "Should this school lower its academic standards in order to keep so many students from 'failing'?" You discuss this with the superintendent of schools.

Or, "Should all girls be required to take the basic course in homemaking, as has been suggested by the school board?" You discuss this with a local woman who manages a highly successful advertising agency.

(3) You interview a well-known person for a "personality" story, so the reader will know as much as possible about him as an individual.

For example: a local poet who has won national recognition —who, you discover, owns a farm in the hills and spends much time there overseeing it; the band director—who is a fishing enthusiast and as a hobby makes artificial lures; the home economics teacher, a petite lady who has made all the furniture in her house, which she designed herself—in a new residential development which she is managing herself, having bought the land years ago.

(4) You interview some visitor who is an interesting and

colorful individual, and tell about him as a visitor whom the reader would like to see.

For example: Perhaps a noted fashion designer visits the campus to look up an old friend; or a television actress is in town for a benefit; or a concert pianist drops in to see his former teacher—these are persons whom the reader would like to see for himself.

In this kind of story, the reader is interested in such matters as how they acted, how they looked, what they wore, and the like.

Sad Comment

The "personality story" is popular in school papers. However, this has degenerated sadly into a kind of stereotyped survey.

Under some such label as Student of the Month, this becomes merely a list of answers which the subject wrote on a questionnaire handed to him. In many cases this includes such items as favorite food, favorite color, favorite song, and so on.

It is often called Personality of the Month—but no hint of this particular individual's personality shows through the listing of his answers. The purpose of these stories should be to show how the person selected differs from others.

In this connection, a contest judge for the South Dakota High School Press Association says, "Many papers fail here. Perhaps the biggest weakness in high school papers running these stories is that the reporter fails to develop the personality of the one being interviewed. The second is that the interview fails to yield specific information about the person."

The Plus Quality

Here, dear writer, is the place where you say to the reader: "Let me show you how the world looks through my glasses!"

For here you tell not only what the interviewee said—but in quoting him you choose words that give the flavor of his language, show how he expresses himself—you tell the reader how the interviewee looked, what kind of person he appeared to be, what gestures he used, what things seemed to be characteristic of him.

You give the setting of the interview. You dramatize. You do everything words will help you do to serve as the looking glass for the reader.

Question Most Important

When the question itself is of primary importance, the persons to answer must be selected carefully. The reader will want to know who is answering and why you chose each one, since the purpose here is to give the reader an idea of a cross section of opinion on this subject.

For a school paper, this kind of interview story is not only practical but also a good way to gain reader interest. Generally speaking, students are interested in what other students are thinking on topics of serious nature. Occasionally this can be turned into a means of getting some humor into the paper. Beware, however, of silly questions and sillier answers.

Serious questions might include the following:

How are students responding to the principal's recent emphasis on "the pursuit of excellence"?

What do students think about the new regulation that no shorts are to be worn on campus?

What is the student response to the police chief's proposal that a teen-age commission be appointed as a part of the traffic safety campaign?

How do students feel about instituting a school court?

Symposium

This kind of story is frequently called the "symposium interview."

Although this sampling of public opinion offers an excellent opportunity for the writer, the story itself can be difficult to do well.

In a study of symposium interviews, R. M. Neal, of the University of Missouri, observed three general faults: (1) the persons interviewed were poorly chosen, (2) the story was clogged with comments too much alike, and (3) "the writing floundered."

Purpose Determines Story

"The interview," it has been said, "is the conversation with a purpose."

The information gained as a result of putting this purpose into action determines the kind of story produced.

As an illustration of the kinds of information sought in interviewing, the following notes may be helpful:

(1) Observable *objective* facts as to conditions or events.

There are two aspects here:

First, a senator is interviewed to learn how he voted on a child labor amendment. (This is an objective fact, regarding which others as well as he can testify, and which can be verified by reference to the *Congressional Record*.)

Second, the senator is interviewed to learn facts of his youthful experience as a field hand in the wheat harvest. (This is equally objective, but is not a matter of record nor obtainable elsewhere.)

(2) *Subjective* facts.

Again two aspects. For example:

The senator is asked his opinion as to whether the business sentiment of the country is strongly hostile to the amendment.

The senator is questioned regarding his attitude toward the desirability of such legislation.

A Final Observation

These definitions and illustrations suggest the limitless possibilities of the interview.

The success of the student, as of the professional, lies in his enthusiasm for his story.

There are techniques to be learned, there are principles to follow—but every story can be a successful story, beginning with your first.

The secret? It is simple:

Start now. Do the very best you can, as soon as you can.

Every story done to the best of your ability is a steppingstone to success.

Chapter IV

STARTING POINT FOR BEGINNERS

"All mankind," said Benjamin Franklin, "is divided into three classes—those that are immovable, those that are movable, and those that move."

This chapter is dedicated to the third group—those that move.

The student journalist, like his professional colleague, must be a person of action. How eagerly he meets the world and how assiduously he studies to develop his techniques determine both the speed and the measure of his success.

When to begin? Now.

Where to begin? There is no better way to get a good start in writing than in learning to interview with skill.

This takes know-how. It takes determination. It takes work.

What Is 'Work'?

In developing ability in interviewing, "work" means taking every opportunity available to practice.

(1) Seek stories. When you have an assignment, find out exactly what is expected. Why is this being written?

(2) Cover each assignment, large or small, so conscientiously that you can say, "This is the very best I can do now."

(3) Develop standards so that you can evaluate your work.

(4) Seek and accept graciously helpful criticism.

To Gain Proficiency

Interviewing is both an art and a skill.

It is based on a thorough understanding that it takes two persons to make a successful interview—but that it is the writer's responsiblity alone to see that it is carried off well.

It consists not in one general ability but in a combination of a great many specific habits, procedures, and techniques.

Many of these habits, procedures, and techniques come only after a period of trial and error. There is no quick substitute for practice.

And yet, it is not time itself that counts in this practice. The important factor is the intensity of your interest in succeeding.

A book like this offers suggestions and helps, provides patterns, utters warnings about problems and pitfalls. It is intended to help the beginner avoid mistakes, teach him how to make the most of his efforts, how to focus on essentials.

Yet, just as a manual entitled *How to Learn to Swim* cannot make you a swimmer, neither can this book make you a successful interviewer. To learn to swim, you must devote yourself to studied effort. The same is true of interviewing.

Once you have gained some competence in basic procedures and have an understanding of your purposes, you begin to see that rules and maxims are meant only as guides—for in any interview there is always room for the play of individuality and initiative.

What you learn in one interview will carry over into another —but no two will ever be exactly alike.

Attracting Attention

"To attract attention you must be different."

This statement was made to a group of student journalists by a speaker at a press meet. He paused and then added, "But different in a nice way."

And what is the best way to be "different"?

"Well, it's this," he declared. "The best way to attract attention by being 'different' is by doing an outstandingly good job, at whatever you're doing."

He really wasn't speaking of interviewing alone, but he might have been. For the reporter who has selected interviewing as his specialty has chosen one of the quickest and surest ways of bringing favorable attention to himself.

Ideas Make a Difference

Had Benjamin Franklin been disposed to say more of his three groups of people, he doubtless would have used the word "ideas" in speaking of the third group—those that move. For the intelligent human being, the one who "moves," is motivated by his ideas.

This is a place where the student journalist is distinguished

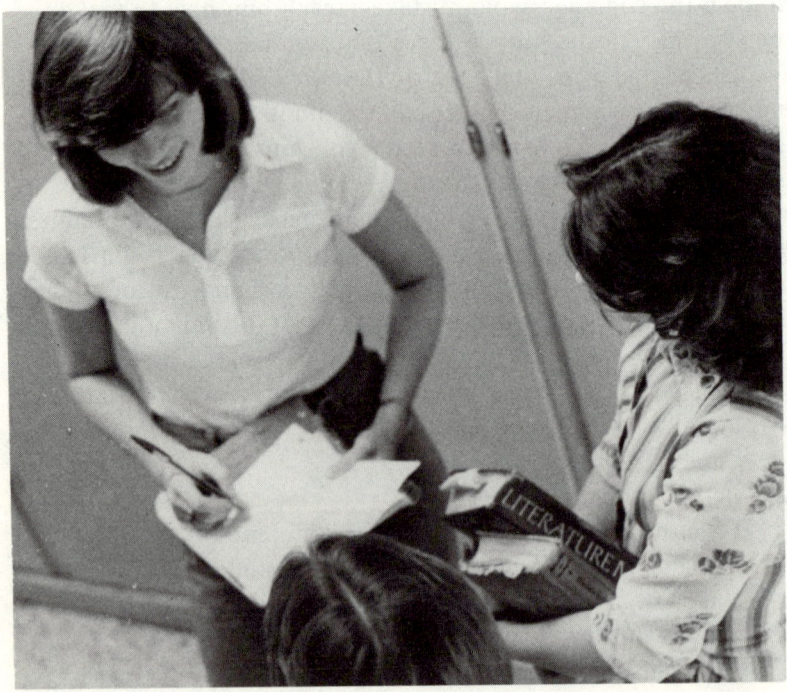

"This would make a good story. Tell me more." The reporter who always has something to write about is interested in what people are saying and doing.

from many of his high school colleagues, for journalism is an area where ideas are basic to all action. And it is the place where he is on common ground with his colleagues who are professionals.

What sweeter words could possibly fall upon an adviser's ears —or what could an editor hope for more—than to hear some staff member say, as he looks up brightly, *"I've got an idea!"*

—"Ideas," which, as Lester Markel, of the *New York Times,* said in addressing a high school press convention, "are the most precious commodity in the world." (However, he went on to add: "But the best and brightest idea in the world is valueless unless it is properly carried into effect.")

To the reporter any discussion of ideas has to do with getting subjects for stories to write. The enthusiastic writer is always looking for story ideas. He may sit down at his typewriter and dash off his idea in a few minutes, or he may file it away in his mind—but he is always on the lookout for bright, fresh story material.

A reporter on the *St. Louis Post-Dispatch,* Francis Albert Behymer, had a way of saying this:

"Methuselah lived 969 years, and all they said about him was that he died. But what was he doing for 969 years? What a story, and all the reporters missed it!"

A Reporter's Rewards

Frequently the "I've got an idea!" has to do with how to get the information, rather than what to write about.

Such was the case with a correspondent for the Associated Press, Eugene Lyons, when he interviewed the Shah of Persia.

The idea for the story itself was simple enough—but getting in to see the Shah was another matter. It took weeks to arrange a meeting, and much strategy.

Lyons' comment on this most unusual opportunity—for the Shah did not care to give audience to newsmen—is a simple statement that in a few calm words indicates what the journalist considers his rewards:

"After the interview, while waiting for the Baku boat, I offhandedly mentioned that I had been an hour with the Shah.

"The news spread through the seaport, and a reporter had an hour of glory on the Southern edge of the Caspian Sea.

"In the larger world, the interview was printed one day, noticed by a few of my friends, and forgotten the next day.

"Only in my own memory it remains edged with excitement."

To Summarize:

Yes, interviewing is basic. Learning to ask the right questions to get the right answers is essential to your success.

It is the key to achievement in journalism.

It is the secret introduction to the excitement of knowing more about the world around you and the people who make it go.

PART TWO

Preparing for the Interview

Chapter V

UNDERSTANDING YOUR ASSIGNMENT

From today's Boy Scouts back to the times of the great orator Demosthenes, the importance of preparation for any endeavor has been underscored.

With the Boy Scouts it is simply "Be Prepared"—a slogan to follow as a kind of way of facing the world.

Of the orations of Demosthenes this was said: "Even his impromptus smell of the lamp." These words, ascribed to Pytheas, may seem a little quaint to us—for we moderns would say, "He believed in burning the midnight oil."

But however we phrase it, the idea is basic: If you expect to succeed—in any job, large or small—you must prepare yourself. You must be prepared.

There is no such thing as competent performance without complete preparation. And the converse is true—encouragingly so for beginners. If you work diligently at complete preparation, you can expect competent performance.

Winner's Luck

"I believe that preparation wins," said J. C. Penney, nationally known as a successful businessman. "A man must know all about his business; he must know a little more than any other man knows. As a rule we achieve what we prepare for. I believe that hard work wins.

"The only kind of *luck* that any man is justified in banking on is hard work, which is made up of sacrifice, persistent and dogged determination."

(Luck, it has been said, is what happens when effort and opportunity meet. Some folks never travel far, because they plan their course by lassitude and loungetude.)

An American Indian preacher-teacher named Andy Dolbow put the idea this way:

"When you are chopping wood and you have a dull axe, you must work all the harder to cut the log. A sharp axe makes work easy—so sharpen your axe all you can."

First Things First

"All right," you say, "I want to prepare myself to be competent at interviewing. What should I do to 'sharpen my axe'?"

Answer: (1) Get your assignment firmly in mind. Know exactly what is expected of you. (2) Work out a story line. (3) Dig for background information. (4) Plan your questions. (5) Make an appointment.

Many of us go about our assignments much like the alumnus who was visiting the college campus for a football game. After standing in line for several minutes, he began to complain about the slow ticket takers at the stadium entrance.

"Whattaya mean, ticket taker?" the man behind him snorted. "This is the line for renting plastic raincoats!"

Assignment Card

In order to have a definite understanding about your assignment, see that you have the assignment written down, with any suggestions or comments the editor or adviser has made.

Most editors have regular assignment cards so both you and he have an exact idea about the story he wants.

The following is typical of what most high school staffs use. It can be easily modified to serve your purposes if you find that other information added here will be helpful to you.

A 3″ × 5″ card is a convenient size.

```
           REPORTER'S ASSIGNMENT—The High Times
         _____Reporter's name
Subject_____
        _____Length    _____Type of story
Sources_____
_____
Special instructions_____
Date due_____  Editor_____
        Date assigned_____
```

Suggestion: You will save yourself time—and possibly embarrassment—if you check the assignment card carefully to see that the names of the interviewees are spelled correctly and that all other information is exact.

Another suggestion: Make *sure* that every time you write a person's name you have it spelled correctly. This insures your spelling it correctly in the last draft of your story and frees you from any last-minute dashing around to check the spelling.

If you check the spelling the first time you use the name—or any word about which you are doubtful—then you are always correct, and you never come out in print with a mistake that makes you look careless or ignorant.

For some strange reason, errors seem to be compounded. Once an error creeps into your story, even though very small, it is likely to persist, or appear elsewhere in different guise. One error seems to lead to another as if with a kind of diabolic glee.

Kinds of Stories

With a little experience, you will discover that stories requiring you to interview one or more persons seem to fall into three groups: the "fact" story, the "people" story, the "idea" story.

The 'Fact' Story

The story where the main interest is in the facts presented may be either a straight news story or a feature.

Who is doing what? Why? Frequently a situation means several story possibilities. For example: A campus club initiates a recreation program for underprivileged children. Three stories—"fact," "people," and "idea."

Here, you are to go in search of information. Your purpose is to find out what happened, or what is happening now, or what is going to happen. When you have this information, you are to write an account that will answer all the Five W's, plus as much background information as time and space will allow.

On the school paper this would include such assignments as interviewing the band director about the new band uniforms, or the Key Club president about the club's recognition banquet, or the chairman of the math department about the new computers to be installed in the math classes as an aspect of experimental studies.

In all stories of this kind, the chief consideration is in the facts that answer the Five W's—who, what, when, where, why—and *how*.

These are objective stories and allow no room for the reporter's subjective response to the situation. They afford no opportunity for creative imagination as we usually think of it.

The effectiveness of this kind of story lies in

(1) the range of information you obtained,
(2) the background you are able to include,
(3) the care with which you worked out the arrangement of the facts,
(4) the impact of the summary lead,
(5) the clearness and simplicity of the writing.

The 'People' Story

The story where the main interest is in the person whom you are interviewing will be a feature story.

Although you are seeking facts, your purpose will be to present those facts in some sort of "warm news" way, as is sometimes said.

Here you will be asking questions for factual answers, but you will be noting as much as possible about the personality and character of the interviewee, as well as something of the setting.

You will be aware of not only what the interviewee says, but how he says it. The reason is that you will want to quote him directly to give as much as possible of the flavor of his conversation. You will note how he looks, what mannerisms he displays, and the like.

The emphasis is not only on *what* in this kind of story but also on *who*.

Such stories as this for the school paper might include an interview with a fellow student who is building a pipe organ in his back yard workshop, or with the girl who is a straight "A" student and who has been throwing papers on a morning paper route for years, or the English instructor who teaches judo in his spare time.

As you ask questions and note the answers, you will experience a subjective response. This will go into your story, for here you have an opportunity for creative imagination.

This kind of story is not only facts, but facts as you see them. The reader wants to know about the person who is related to the facts you are presenting.

The effectiveness of this kind of story lies in

(1) the interest of the story idea you have selected,

(2) the enthusiasm which you evidence for the subject,

(3) the quality of your creative imagination—that is, the way you dramatize the interview for your reader, complete with setting and characterization,

(4) the skill with which you translate your enthusiasm into words so the reader can experience the same pleasure you feel.

The 'Idea' Story

In many stories, especially for adult readers, the main interest is in the ideas, thoughts or opinions of the person or persons interviewed.

Stories of this kind are not very common in school papers. One reason is that more space is needed here than most papers can afford. Also, generally, student readers are more interested in people than in ideas.

Many papers, however, make effective use of this kind of

story by asking an individual whose opinion would be considered worthwhile a question of widespread or deep interest to the student body.

Such questions might be something like these:

How could the student council constitution be amended to allow more representation of the home rooms?

What improvements could be suggested for the present report card system?

What do the business leaders in the community expect of the schools, specifically?

Would a 12-month school year solve the need for more classroom space in the local school system?

The effectiveness of this kind of story lies in

(1) The care with which the ideas to be presented are isolated and developed,

(2) the clarity of the writing.

Assigned or Otherwise

As a beginning reporter, you will cover stories that are assigned you by the editor.

Very soon, however, if you are interested in writing for the paper, you will begin to see story ideas.

Then you can volunteer for a story, or you can write it and submit it to your editor. (Among your older colleagues in the writing business, this is called free lancing.)

For example:

You journey over to the band room to get information for a story about the spring concert. As you walk in the door, you see the band director holding up a new uniform. You soon discover that he is showing the kind of new uniform the band will be wearing next year. This gives you an idea for a story, on new uniforms. Who decides? Who pays for them?

Also, you hear him say that attractive uniforms do something for a band's morale.

Idea: You query him about this, then see other faculty members on factors in morale building.

Idea: You see a coin collector's book on his desk and recall that you have heard that he is interested in numismatics. You ask about this, discover enough material for a long story about his coin collection, even attend a coin auction with him.

Idea: Did someone say that faculty members aren't interested in anything but homework and tests?

Chapter VI

WORKING OUT A STORY LINE

Unity and impact are elements of a story that is well designed and well built from the beginning.

Consequently, it is essential that you get your story off to a good start.

In an assignment for a news story, you have the Five W's as a guide for gathering and organizing information.

If, however, your assignment is not a straight news story, some thinking is necessary on your part before you are ready to delve into background study or dash off for an interview.

This thinking is to help you establish a "story line."

Your questions must be related to a central idea. Your planning must be guided by a controlling purpose.

This is the point at which the unity of your story fails or succeeds.

The story line that underlies your preliminary planning is the secret to a successful lead, which in turn is the secret to a successful headline—all of which contributes to the impact of your story.

If you expect your writing to have unity, you must "think unified."

Working It Out

For example:

An exchange student from Norway enters your school in November. You decide to interview him for a story. With no thought for a story line, you dash off, catch him between classes and pop a few questions such as: How do you like this campus? What are your favorite Mexican foods? What do you think of

American teen-agers? What do teen-agers in your country do on dates?

Sounds familiar, doesn't it?

Yes, because in school papers you see innumerable write-ups (we purposely refrain from calling them stories, since by definition they are *not* stories) that are about as haphazardly put together as this.

Need we say that this is *not* the way to do?

Now consider:

You hear about the exchange student from Norway. You see that there is a story possibility here—somewhere.

You turn this over in your mind, seeking some idea that will give you a story line. It would help to know more about him, background and the like, so you visit the dean to see what general information you can find to afford some suggestions.

The dean doesn't seem to know much, but after a few minutes you have learned that (1) he is interested in music, plays an instrument—a zither, of all things, (2) he has been a junior counselor at a camp for small boys and (3) he is very serious about doing well in his studies and about representing his country favorably.

With this much information, you make an opportunity to meet him, your purpose still being to try to find a story idea. In general conversation with him and others, you discover some interesting things about him:

(1) He would like to see some *real* Indians ("like those on television.") (2) He is delighted with "American" food—such as pizza, hot tamales. (3) He is an expert oarsman. (4) He enjoys reading Edgar Allan Poe. (5) He has just bought his mother a Christmas present.

Next Step

You tell him that you would like to do a story about him for the paper and make an appointment for an interview. Then you go off to a quiet place and *think*.

As your mind travels back over the various comments made,

Working Out a Story Line

you jot down ideas for possible story lines. Your notes would be something like this:

1. Interested in music . . . plays a zither. (Music is a universal language: *idea.*) Says he likes to perform for groups, will get acquainted this way. Is he especially fond of some particular kind of music, folk, etc.?

Research for your assignment sometimes leads you on an extensive storeroom safari. Who but a fellow journalist would know how exultant you feel when you finally climb the filing cabinet and can reach for the record book you need?

2. Junior counselor for small boys. What kind of camp?
3. Hopes to do well in his studies?
4. Hopes to be a good ambassador for his country, is enthusiastic about the exchange program. *Idea:* How does the exchange program work? Just exactly how does one get to be considered for this? What did he have to do? How much of this is his individual responsibility?
5. See *real* Indians . . . What a teacher television is! *Idea!*
6. "American" food—pizza! *Idea:* What does "American" mean?
7. Expert oarsman . . . Norwegian sports . . .
8. Christmas present for his mother . . . wonder what he bought. What is Christmas like in Norway? In an average Norwegian family? . . . detailed story about this might be interesting . . . what is typical . . . different . . .

This probing of your thoughts—plus the actual writing of your ideas as you consider your various items of information—is basic to your success as a reporter and writer.

No Cheating Here
There is no way to cheat on this. And no one else can do it for you.
The enthusiasm and intensity with which you work at this beginning will in great measure determine your success.

Developing Ideas
You decide on two or three possibilities and develop these ideas:
1. John Olsson is walking proof that music is a universal language.
2. John Olsson tells step by step how the exchange program works.
3. John Olsson adds his bit in definition of "American."
4. How would John Olsson be observing Christmas if he were

home, home being a village in northern Norway where his father is engaged in a boat service?

You consider these possibilities—and you add another:

5. John Olsson is a person of many talents, many accomplishments, very popular—a delightful and successful ambassador from his country. What makes him tick? . . .

To Summarize:

The foregoing illustrates what we mean when we say that you begin by trying to find a story line that pleases you.

Now you are in a position to do research that will contribute to your total idea and to plan questions that will form a complete and significant story. It does not matter so much which story line you choose as that you do choose and that you then stay with it.

Chapter VII

SEEKING BACKGROUND INFORMATION

"The beforehand is what makes the difference."
Whoever first uttered this statement should be presented a Medal of Special Recognition for Stating Basic Ideas in Simple Phrases by all student journalists endeavoring to succeed in interviewing.

The beforehand . . .

This means, of course, getting your background information.

And getting background information means making every effort to find out as much as possible about your subject before you interview him.

There is no predetermined set of helps that will aid you as much as your own lively interest in your subject. Your purpose is to learn about the subject so you can work out a story line and then plan questions designed to get information for a story built on that story line.

No one can be expected to help you as much as you can help yourself. As always in this business of writing, you are your own best assistant—or your own worst enemy. You either help yourself succeed, or you defeat yourself.

However, it does help to know where to begin—and so—

Visit the Library
The library, both the school library and the city library, can almost always come to your rescue. If you are not acquainted and do not feel at ease in looking for material yourself, take courage and ask the librarian for assistance.

Tell her what you would like to know. (If you don't know what you want, then tell her what your story is and ask her what help she can suggest.) Librarians wish to be of service and they are trained to find answers to questions.

Reference helps include the various encyclopedias, *Current Biography,* the *Reader's Guide to Periodical Literature,* and the like. In addition, there are many reference books on specific subjects.

As a beginning journalist, you would be wise to visit the library to see for yourself just what kind of helps are available. In the reference section, take time to study the shelves carefully. Later, then, you will have a better idea of what information the library offers.

In addition to books, there are magazine files, pamphlet files, and clipping files—all catalogued and indexed so you can run down various items as easily as possible. Again, here the librarian will try to help you if she can. And here again, you must ask her, or she will not know that you want her assistance.

For example:

Suppose you are to interview the president of the new Gun Collectors Club regarding a city-wide exhibit of old guns. Before the interview, in a quick survey of the information in the encyclopedia, you note a paragraph about dueling pistols. Later, during your interview, you find that the president is going to display a set of dueling pistols he found in a junk shop.

After a little inquiry, you dash back to the library to check up on a hazy recollection of a picture somewhere. And you're right. The president's dueling pistols are likely to be the oldest and most valuable in the exhibit—about eighteenth century, French. Looking further, you find that this kind of pistol was among the weapons found recently in a cache of loot on the Gulf Coast. With a few deft strokes, you now give special flavor to this story.

This may not be earth shaking, but it does indicate that even a little background information can add a dash of sparkle and color to your writing. (Not only because it is a colorful fact in itself, but because it interests you—and what interests you will

The reference section in the journalism department should be as complete as possible, for finding the right book means finding the answers to questions that have to be answered. Every young writer will want to begin assembling books for his own reference shelf. These include a dictionary, a thesaurus, know-how-to-do-it helps, and collections of "model" stories and ideas.

interest your reader, for your enthusiasm is transmitted to him through the words you write.)

Classroom Reference

Every newspaper office should have a reference shelf. If your newspaper is very rich and is housed in spacious quarters, then your reference shelf might well be a reference room, complete with all the reference helps any of the staff will ever need.

However, most of our school papers are not very rich and do not occupy spacious quarters. In fact, many of them are fortunate to have any money at all and to occupy even a room that they can call their own. Many simply have to do the best they can about their budget and share a desk in one corner of the room in which their adviser teaches a full schedule of classes during the day.

This would be very sad, except that where there is the wit and the will to win, there is usually a happy solution.

For example:

One adviser and her staff decided to provide themselves with a reference library. After careful study, they selected their books and magazines and then faced the problem of where to put them, as the room was small and crowded.

They solved their problem by buying a small metal table with shelves and on rollers, the kind used in many libraries. One of the boys later suggested that he could make one similar to this in the woodworking shop—and he did.

The metal table was reserved for books. The other held the magazines to which they subscribed, the newspaper file for the preceding year, the "stick" holding issues of the current year to date, the most recent volume of the yearbook, the scrapbook, and a box containing the pamphlet file and the clipping file.

This story really has another ending to this ending:

At a recent meeting of journalism advisers when this story was told about the "rolling bookshelf," one adviser spoke up happily.

"You've given me an *idea!*" she said, beaming. "My problem is that I am a 'floating' teacher, so I have to meet my newspaper staff in a room which is also used by typing classes. Therefore, we can have nothing stored in their room. This idea of the rolling table will solve my problems, for we can store all our supplies, books, materials, and the like on the table—and then roll it down the hall for our journalism period. As a 'floating adviser,' I'll equip a 'floating office' for the staff."

Titles Suggested

You will want to buy as many books and subscribe to as many publications as your budget will allow. In selecting reference books, consider which you will use the most and which will be the best buys for your money. Remember that your school library has a reference section available, so you will want to supplement volumes there.

If possible, you should have an unabridged dictionary conveniently placed for the quickest possible reference. (Webster's is a favorite.) Other volumes would include as many books on usage as you can acquire, a thesaurus, a book of synonyms, a book showing how to divide words, a standard desk book, a state almanac, and as many books in special fields as can be obtained.

And Other Helps

Actually, your reference section should include anything you think would be of help to anyone on the staff at any time.

Much of this information can be compiled by the staff over a period of time. This is an important aid in building up background information for your particular situation.

(1) Maintain a file covering general subjects, such as Administration; Guidance; Student Council; Curriculum; Chartered Clubs; and the like.

(2) Ask teachers to fill in information sheets and then file these. As you find additional items of interest, add these, stapling them to the proper sheet.

(3) See that all clubs send you their statistics and other information you would need, such as purposes, plans, officers.

(4) Maintain a complete directory of the student body by hav-

ing each student fill out a card with his name, address, telephone number, home room, class and schedule. This is most convenient if kept on 3" × 5" cards, alphabetized.

Called a Morgue

This "bureau of editorial reference" is usually called a morgue. It is a specific body of materials, located in a specific place in a newspaper office so it is easily and readily accessible.

If you have a filing cabinet, you can keep clippings, pamphlets, letters, and the like sorted, organized and filed. The success of this depends on the person in charge. He must see that the cabinet is kept in order, with all materials properly filed after they are used.

Every staff member is expected to do his part in keeping the file in proper order.

If you do not have a filing cabinet, you can sort and organize the material you want to keep and then arrange it in folders properly labeled or in large envelopes. Many staffs prefer the envelopes, since papers will not fall out.

Then arrange these folders or envelopes in a box that will conveniently accommodate them. Though this may sound like a makeshift, it can be kept neat and look businesslike and attractive. It has the added advantage of portability.

A scrapbook is another help. This, too, depends on the care with which it is compiled. It is satisfactory to take a large looseleaf notebook and on theme paper, or paper cut to size, paste clippings from local and state papers concerning activities and persons connected with your school.

This is convenient if kept chronologically, but it could be divided into departments or sections. All clippings should be dated and the source indicated. On the cover and backbone put the dates included. If one book is filled before the year ends, begin another. As the years move on, your office has an invaluable source of information about the school activities as recorded by the papers.

Your reference section should also include the bound files of your newspaper as far back as possible. Many schools now are keeping their files on microfilm. This, however, is more for safekeeping than for frequent use. It is convenient to have bound files in the journalism room where they can be referred to easily.

Preserve Your Files

Caution: One complete set of files should be maintained by the paper and preserved. This file should never be available for general use, because volumes are likely to be damaged or lost.

A complete file of the school yearbook, also, should be maintained by the school paper. This, like the newspaper, should be two sets of files. One set should be maintained by the office, preserved, and never checked out. A second set should be available for student use, with the provision that each volume is to be checked out and checked in carefully. Yearbooks are often lost or damaged by clipping.

Somewhere in the office there should be a place for odds and ends of information that come in from time to time. Gradually these can be filed where they will be most helpful.

Wise is the staff member who does his part in maintaining the morgue, for he will appreciate the convenience of having material easily accessible for background information.

People Help Too

In looking for background information, you will find that sometimes other persons can help you.

For example:

You are going to interview a boy in the printing department about a four-year scholarship he has been awarded by a publishing house. Since the printing instructor wrote a letter of recommendation for the boy, you know that he will be able to give you something for your "beforehand."

You expect to write a story about a student in the art department who has had some paintings selected for a traveling art show. Before interviewing the artist, you visit the art instructor for background about the student's work.

Dig, Dig, Dig

In some ways getting ready to do an interview is like getting ready to plant a garden. The word for both is *dig*. Your "beforehand" means digging for all the background possible so that your questions will be planned to help you get the most information possible from your interviewee—and get it related to your story line.

Such "beforehand" will also make you aware and alert, so that if the interviewee says something that might indicate another story, you will be quick to catch this and adeptly ask other questions following this new lead.

"One lesson we can learn in depth is the lesson of lavish preparation," commented Charles Ferguson, of the *Reader's Digest*, speaking to a group of writers at a conference.

"I use the word lavish advisedly because I mean to suggest habits of work that go far beyond the merely necessary, so that the task at hand gets deep into the mind and conscience. *Any piece of copy worth troubling about is worth a good deal of study.*"

Chapter VIII

PLANNING QUESTIONS

You wouldn't try to make a cake without a recipe.

Or attempt to put the pieces of a model airplane together without an instruction sheet.

Or set forth on an extensive automobile journey without a map marked with your projected itinerary.—Not if you expected to accomplish maximum results in a minimum of time with a minimum of effort.

And in launching upon an interview, you would not attempt to visit the interviewee without a set of questions designed specifically to accomplish your purpose.

Having worked out your story line and gained your background information, you are ready to plan the questions you will ask.

Whether you have only a few minutes' notice or all the time you want, *never depend on luck.*

With skillful questioning, you can guide the conversation so your purposes will be met and you can obtain the information you seek for the story you have in mind.

If you have gained sufficient background information, your questions will fall into place rather naturally as you consider your story line.

Checklist Is Helpful

Although there is no fixed approach to interviews in general, it will help you learn to do professional work by following these principles suggested by professional journalists:

(1) Do I know exactly what I expect to accomplish in this interview? (Try to summarize your story line in one complete

sentence. Add possible related ideas. If you cannot do this, your thinking lacks unity.)

(2) Do I have sufficient questions to cover this? (Write down your questions. Do not expect to depend on your memory.)

(3) What would my readers want to know about this subject? What would they ask if they had an opportunity to interview this person?

(4) Am I prepared to follow the interviewee if he talks rapidly? Am I prepared to coax him on if he tends to be reticent and possibly even avoids direct answers? Am I prepared to guide him if he does not know how to answer the questions? (Most persons are willing to co-operate when you interview them for a story. However, they generally do not know how to give you information or what information to supply and therefore depend on you to guide the conversation.)

(5) Have I planned several approaches so I will not be caught unprepared? Have I anticipated possible difficulties?

(6) Have I planned for all possible angles as I see them from here?

(7) Am I prepared to take advantage of additional angles that might show up?

(8) Am I prepared to take advantage of additional time if the interviewee offers to continue the conversation?

Make an Appointment

One of the last phases of your preparation for your interview is to make an appointment. Courtesy and efficiency demand this.

Appointments may be made in a number of ways. The most common approaches among professional people are by telehone, by note, or by letter of introduction from a friend. For student journalists, however, often an appointment can be made by speaking with the interviewee and deciding upon a time convenient for both of you.

By having an appointment, you gain confidence, for you know that your idea has been accepted and you know that the time is satisfactory for the interviewee. Also, you are able to save time by seeing the interviewee promptly and by cutting down on preliminary explanations. By having an appointment, you can judge how much time you can take and how to spend it to best advantage.

Furthermore, knowing that he has an interview with you at a definite time regarding a definite subject, the interviewee has opportunity to consider what he may say.

Resourcefulness Needed

Making appointments is usually not much of a problem for student journalists, since they operate in an area where most people are willing to co-operate.

Professional journalists, however, often encounter major difficulties in trying to see those whom they want to interview. Their procedures range from the most daring battle strategy to the diplomat's subtlest wiles and guiles.

Lisa Hobbs, of the *San Francisco Examiner,* gambled against heavy odds to manage to get information about Red China. Posing as an Australian tourist, she was the first staff reporter of a United States newspaper to enter mainland China in almost ten years.

A different kind of story is told about an interview with George Bernard Shaw.

S. J. Woolf, an artist working with a New York magazine, while on a visit in London had tried without success to get past Shaw's secretaries to gain an interview.

Finally, on July 1, he wrote Shaw the following note:

"My dear Mr. Shaw—Years ago I remember you said that the only reason you posed for Rodin was because you felt that it was the one way in which you could gain everlasting fame. That is quite true as far as Europe is concerned—but as for America, with true Shavian modesty, I may say that immortality will not be yours until I have drawn you. That is one of the reasons why I came to London—to obtain immortality for you in America. And when you think it will cost you only one-half hour of time, that is a very small price to pay."

The following morning Woolf received this note from Shaw:

"I now have considerable experience as an artist's model; but my terms—about $3,750 an hour—are prohibitive. Also, I shall not be disengaged for at least a year to come."

Whereupon Woolf drafted this:

"My dear Mr. Shaw—Your price for posing is acceptable to me. My price for drawing is the same amount. You do not have to be disengaged while I draw. I am leaving on the eighth. When shall I come? If you could pose this afternoon, and sign the drawing today, think what it would mean to the American people to have two vital documents on July Fourth."

He got the interview.

Chapter IX

WHAT YOU SHOULD KNOW ABOUT PEOPLE

Aheadability.

This word is a newcomer to the English language. A certain advertising agency claims to have coined it in reference to the manufacturer of a new hay-making machine invented in the mid-sixties.

"Aheadability—the knack of being first with the finest for farmers," the advertisement says.

It is a very descriptive word in relation to hay makers.

And equally descriptive in relation to story makers.

Aheadability—the knack of getting yourself into your story the best way possible the soonest way possible.

Understanding Others

One secret to getting into your story quickly and well has to do with people. The more you can learn about people and the way they behave, the more you are able to work with them easily and with understanding.

There are several philosophies popular today concerning the way to get along with people. Some insist that you develop a sneaky approach in order to get what you want from others. Some advise browbeating; some advise a kind of honey tone— but you will discover that nothing succeeds like a genuine interest in people as individuals.

You need not struggle for a "line" or a "front." If you sincerely like people, they are immediately disposed to like you.

No guile, no subterfuge are necessary. Your sincerity is apparent. It is charming, even often disarming. People want to be liked—and they like you if they think you like them. It is that simple.

What You Should Know About People

Why Study Psychology?

"Psychology" is a commodity on the market today. You often hear advice about studying psychology.

A quick summary of this advice is offered by Carl R. Rogers, University of Chicago psychologist. He says:

Do you want to understand people? Then

(1) Always try to see the interviewee's behavior as it appears to him.

(2) Observe "uncontrolled behavior patterns"—i.e., watch people everywhere.

(3) Be alive to the meanings which make people act the way they do.

(4) Listen in on conversations of others.

If you want to improve your psychological know-how, then be aware of the deeper meanings of conversation. Study behavior articles on psychology. Develop the power of "listening with understanding."

Summary: The more you understand about the general patterns of behavior, the more easily you can predict another's responses and reactions. Hence, you are better prepared to get along with him, whether in an interiew, or a business transaction or merely in an interim of pleasant conversation.

Our Basic Needs

Many volumes have been written on human behavior, and the journalist can learn much from studying them.

But there's an old-fashioned approach to the subject—simple, direct, effective. It brings success and thus it brings satisfaction.

To Feel Important

First, a person needs to feel important, feel that he counts for something, that his efforts are worth while. This is a feeling that he must have about himself.

If you understand this, then when you interview him, you realize that in your approach you must let him know that you think his story is worth telling.

The very fact that you want to see him about a story means that you think he has a story to tell—but he doesn't necessarily realize this.

If you really consider him important to your story and thus to you and your reader, then let him know this. Show it by the questions you ask. Plan leading questions that help you get yourself in step with him.

Ask—and then *listen*.

One of the greatest questions in the language is this: *"And then, what did you do next?"*

To Be Appreciated

The second deep need that people feel is a need for appreciation. This is a feeling in which you are related to him. He is satisfied in this only when he senses a response in you.

Never be guilty of thinking that this can be a kind of act put on or off at will. The truth will show. You appreciate him and what he is doing—or you don't appreciate him. Real appreciation comes from the heart.

Not long ago a large manufacturing company employed a new sales director who issued a decree that in the course of one week every staff member would have said at least one word of appreciation to every other member.

This was a complete failure. Not only did it turn into a kind of joke, but everyone sensed that the idea made light of a deep-seated human need. (A need, incidentally, that has two aspects. We not only want to be appreciated, we want to express our sense of appreciation to others.) A sales director simply cannot legislate appreciation.

There is a kind of "fringe benefit" here, for appreciation of what others are doing shifts your attention from yourself to others.

As you make a conscious effort to look for things you can appreciate in other people, your personality is improved, and you gain confidence as you gain understanding.

To Be Liked by Others

Being liked—an idea that is scoffed at now and then in certain circles, of both the young and the not so young. But do not be misled by this.

You will succeed in getting along with people only if you believe that others want to be liked and if you make every effort to show them that you like them. Also, to succeed, *you must do your best to make yourself likable.*

Getting along with people is a two-way relationship. However, since you are taking the initiative, it is you who must make the effort. As the writer, it is you who guide the interview, control the meeting.

There is no sure way for you to *appear* to like the other person—unless you really do. Of course, there are some people whom we simply do not care for, just as there are others whom we enjoy being with. It is hard to explain these feelings.

Perhaps it is well enough to recognize them—and then as writers make every effort to find at least something to like about even those whom we consider generally "unlikable."

Understanding Yourself

What you should know about yourself may pose more of a problem than what you should know about others.

Actually, you are a very important person.

Determination Counts

You can succeed if you want to. Determination will carry you through many a situation—even a crisis—where ability may fail you.

The psychologists use a term for this—D.Q. They say that your intelligence quotient is your I.Q.—your achievement quotient is your A.Q.—and your *drive quotient* is your D.Q.

The D.Q. is frequently more important to one's total accomplishment than is his I.Q. or his A.Q.

Pleasing Personality

You can improve your personality, your manners, your total image—if you want to. There are books to read, advisers to consult with—and your own good common sense to help you become a more pleasing person socially.

In this day of the beatnik fads, it is easy to think that these attitudes are general. But be not fooled. The good old-fashioned traits of cleanliness, neatness, attractive attire are still appealing.

As a reporter, especially, it is important to appear to be in command of yourself and present a neat and trim appearance to the public, for this inspires their confidence in you.

No successful business executive, for example, is going to bother to give any of his time to an interview with a teen-ager (or with any other person, for that matter) who slouches in, behaves like a bumpkin, and is unpleasing to look at and listen to.

Such a character may be intelligent, but the executive never finds it out. He doesn't care. He just isn't interested. He has no respect for your story idea and no confidence in your ability to handle it.

A True Story:

In a recent workshop, where this question of appearance came up, one of the school editors present said that he had a "testimonial" to offer.

"I was elected a sports editor," he explained, "and so had to interview the coaches frequently. Right away I began to sense that something was wrong and consequently began to be very self-conscious. I tried to be courteous and do all I thought I was supposed to do, but there was a hidden hostility there. I could just feel it."

He smiled wryly. "Of course, I figured they just didn't like me and was about to let it go at that. However, it wasn't long before I happened to overhear the dean say, 'Coach Masters sees red every time one of these long haircuts darkens his door!'

"Now, I'm not too bright maybe, but I figured that one out. Simple. The coach just didn't like my hair. I guess I surprised him. Because I had it cut. And now any time I need anything from the coaches, I get it. It sure paid off. I've got a press pass to all the athletic events—and I feel welcome in their office any time. They co-operate with the paper just fine."

Fire Up the Sparkle

Your enthusiasm is one of your greatest assets.

There is no way for you to appear interested and enthusiastic unless you really are interested and enthusiastic.

"Nothing is so contagious as enthusiasm," wrote Edward G. Bulwer-Lytton, well-known English author. "It moves stones; it charms brutes."

(Now as a reporter you do not anticipate interviewing stones and brutes—but you never know!)

Psychological tests have proved that enthusiasm releases energy.

In fact, what we call fatigue is mostly boredom. Experiments conducted by the Harvard Fatigue Laboratory indicated that in 90 per cent of the cases studied, fatigue was nothing more than mental boredom.

Boredom, of course, is a word unknown to a busy reporter. Everything he sees, every person he meets, every idea he encounters is exciting and new. His day is a sequence of actions and reactions threaded together by a boundless zest for living.

You're a Somebody

Even the youngest student journalist should understand that the ability to write has always been held in great esteem. Great writers have helped tell the story of mankind. They have served not only as recorders but as prophets and idealists.

Many writers today, of course, put words on the market in a kind of dreadful negation of man and society—but they are hardly more than wordmongers, guilty of abuse and distortion of any ability they may have.

Not all student journalists are going to become great writers. Some will. However, any experience in learning to express yourself in words on paper will help you. And, as you see your stories in print, you may well be proud of your efforts.

Never in the history of the world has the need for communication been so great. Never has the need for intelligence and integrity in writers been so desperate.

Whether your part in this be large or small, it is a significant part—and you are a Somebody.

PART THREE

Conducting the Interview

Chapter X

THE OPENING MOMENTS

Every interview has its zero hour—the point at which the preparation ends and the actual encounter between the interviewer and the interviewee begins.

No matter how brief or perfunctory the questioning, you want to make a good beginning and a good impression, for small interviews are training ground for more important ones, and success in slight interviews lays a foundation for success in more significant ones.

Note well: Here you are your own trainer.

Consider Your Appearance

Whether you are going to be with the interviewee five minutes or an hour, your appearance and manner are important, for you are the center of his attention for that length of time.

He judges you first by the way you look. If you are simply dressed and neat, he is more likely to think of you as a good student and a careful worker than if you arrive in a bizarre outfit or look as if you had slept in your clothes.

To present an acceptable appearance is an effective way to make as favorable a first impression as possible and thus to get your interview off to a good start.

Many a professional reporter has a quick-shoeshine kit in his desk drawer so he can dash off to his interview feeling confident that his shoes won't be a telltale sign of carelessness and indifference. And every girl reporter has a tiny "beauty bar" hidden back somewhere, so she can touch up her hair or freshen her make-up before meeting the public. Why? Because these men and women know that appearance is important. They have learned also that knowing you look your best gives you confidence—and confidence helps spell success.

(The following story is reprinted with permission. Copyright by the *Quill*.)

Keith Fuller, AP assistant general manager, recalls that very soon after he arrived at his first AP assignment, in New Orleans, he began to receive the best reporting assignments.

Aware of his cub status and the experience and ability of the other staffers, he remained puzzled for some time, then finally asked the bureau manager.

The deflating answer was simple: "Fuller, you always wear a tie and jacket."

Consider Your Manners

Your interviewee also judges you by the way you behave. Rudeness never pays, we all know. Many of us do not know that there are other kinds of bad manners that work toward our defeat in various hidden ways. A person interested in creating a favorable impression constantly watches himself to make sure that his conduct is socially acceptable.

This means no chewing gum, no interruptions, no yawning, no raucous voice, no mannerisms that are distracting or displeasing. Why? Because these hinder a congenial relationship between the interviewer and the interviewee.

Teen-agers (and adults, too) who shrug off (or even rebel at) the opportunity to learn social manners because they have a right to be free to do what they please do not understand that social practices are acceptable or unacceptable only in so far as they make you pleasing or unpleasing to be with.

Since you are making an effort to be with the interviewee and want him to co-operate with you, it is obviously to your advan-

The Opening Moments

tage to be as socially acceptable in your behavior as you know how.

That is, you want to be pleasing enough that he will answer your questions and give you the information you seek.

Consider Your Language

Watch what you say. This means to use the correct word in the correct place in the correct grammatical construction.

Your appearance and your manners constitute the basis for

Good grooming gives you confidence. Many successful adults who must look and feel at their best at all times keep a few necessities stored inconspicuously on a shelf in the cabinet or tucked away in the desk.

the first impression you make on others. It is when you open your mouth to speak that you either seal your own doom or you begin to carry your banner high.

Let others scoff at correctness if they like, or lapse into carelessness. But remember this: *You* are trying to make a good impression for *yourself,* and no one can do that except *you.* Set your standards high and then devote your attention to trying to meet them.

The higher you set your standards the better, for you will in that way identify yourself as one who cares.

Punctuality Counts, Too

Your interviewee judges you also by the way you arrive for the meeting. Since most interviews are set up by appointment, it is important for you to be there at the designated time. This means *the* time—not early, not late. It means *exactly* on time.

A word of warning: Be sure that the time for the interview is very clearly stated and that both you and the interviewee are aware of this time. Carelessness here can be a serious troublemaker.

Also, be sure that the meeting place is clearly stated, and that you know where this is. In some instances, you should go early and make certain that you can find the office or room designated.

For example:

Suppose you are to interview some visiting Brazilians who are here buying horses during the auction. You make an appointment—through a Portuguese teacher—to interview them at the stockyard gate, promptly at one o'clock, as they are leaving soon after.

You arrive eager and happily prepared with questions—only to discover that the stockyards cover 90 acres and there are five gates.

Or, suppose you are to see the gym teacher during the five-minute passing period between classes to check on a note about the new officers of the Pep Club just before the paper goes to press. You arrive—and miss her—because you assumed she would be in the gym, but she was in her office checking on game equipment.

Knock before Entering
"I never know when to knock."
If this is your problem, follow this suggestion:
Always knock before entering if the door is closed, unless there is a sign that says "Come in" or some such statement that means that visitors are expected. It is correct to go into a reception room without knocking but never into a private office.
If the door is open, do not enter without knocking if it is obviously a private office.

Introducing Yourself
Even though you have an appointment, and so have reason to feel that the interviewee would know who you are, it is correct to introduce yourself. Note: Always speak distinctly in order to be sure that you are understood and that your name will be repeated correctly.
One sure way to get your interviewee off to a bad start is to confuse him about your name so he does not know how to address you. You can help him feel easy and confident if you make your introduction smooth and clear so he comprehends all the information you need to give him.
Remember: He is not so well acquainted with all the information as you are, so any help you can give him (tactfully, of course) will make it possible for you to get along better with him.
For example:
You have made an appointment with the band director to get information about the forthcoming Christmas concert. You are to meet him in his office adjoining the band room.
Although his door is open, you knock at the door and pause for him to invite you in. You know him but doubt that he knows you, so you say, "Good afternoon, Mr. Burton. I am Tom Shaver,

the High Times reporter who called you about a story on the concert for our next issue."

He says something like, "Yes, Tom, I'm glad you came. We would like to have a story about the program. How can I help you?"

Having already been by the print shop to pick up a copy of the program, you are prepared to ask additional questions for which answers can be obtained only by talking with him. So you say something like this: "We have a copy of the program but would like to give some background information about the soloists and student conductor. . . ."

Liking People

Whether we admit it or not, all of us really want to make a good impression on the people we meet.

In interviewing, if we want to succeed, we must do more than *want* to make a good impression. We must take advantage of every opportunity to help ourselves. Along with all the rules and suggestions, we must remember that it is our inner person that really counts. Our basic attitudes and feelings are bound to show.

If you want to be liked, the Key to Success is surprisingly simple. Deceptively so, you may think.

It is this: "The easiest way to make people like you at once is to develop a genuine and sincere interest in people."

Note that: *genuine . . . sincere . . . interest . . . people.*

A warm, friendly interest in a person for his own sake will carry you through a problem situation much more easily than any amount of clever contriving to get "in."

If you want a person to like you immediately, let him feel that you are favorably impressed with *him*. This is not an artificial approach. It is not a "line."

Just open your eyes and your mind—and *see* him. Then let him know that you like what you see. If you feel this, it will show. You do not have to search for some clever way to put this into words.

For one thing, *listen* to him. Listen with interest. This leads to two results you will find. One is the pleasure of pleasing people by paying attention to what they have to say. The other is learning something you didn't know.

Developing You-ability

This interest in people leads to a better understanding of them and their possible responses and reactions. It is frequently called you-ability. To develop this you-ability is to improve your relationships with people and to increase your pleasure in your associations.

Chapter XI

KEEPING THE INTERVIEWEE TALKING

An interview has been defined as a conversation with a purpose. We might add that it is a controlled conversation.

Is there any foolproof strategy to insure success in controlling this conversation? No.

If you have prepared carefully and are armed with a set of questions following a definite story line, you might well feel that you have done your part. But no. The complete responsibility is yours. To have the questions is one thing. To get full answers in the depth you need is something else.

One of your major problems, therefore, is to keep the interviewee talking. The question is: How?

Procedures Vary

One editor in Washington, D.C. says, "You either kick information out of people or charm it out of them."

It's much simpler than that, others say.

"I just ask direct questions, and usually get direct answers," remarks Ernie Deane, of the *Arkansas Gazette*. "People will answer most of your questions most of the time if they know what you want."

One of the secrets is to learn how to approach the interviewee from the point of view of his own interests, telling him frankly what you want to know and showing how your story will be to his advantage.

To accomplish this, of course, you will have to study your approach to every interview and try to evaluate it. You can be your own best critic.

Others can give you advice and offer to tell you what procedures they employ to gain certain results, but as in learning to paddle a canoe or to swim or to sing, you must *do*—and do with conscious effort and understanding. You must care, care enough to try to find out what works best and then practice—practice and practice and practice.

Another secret:

Point out that you want to be sure that the interviewee understands your purpose. Generally the interviewee will be frank when he feels that his point of view is appreciated and respected

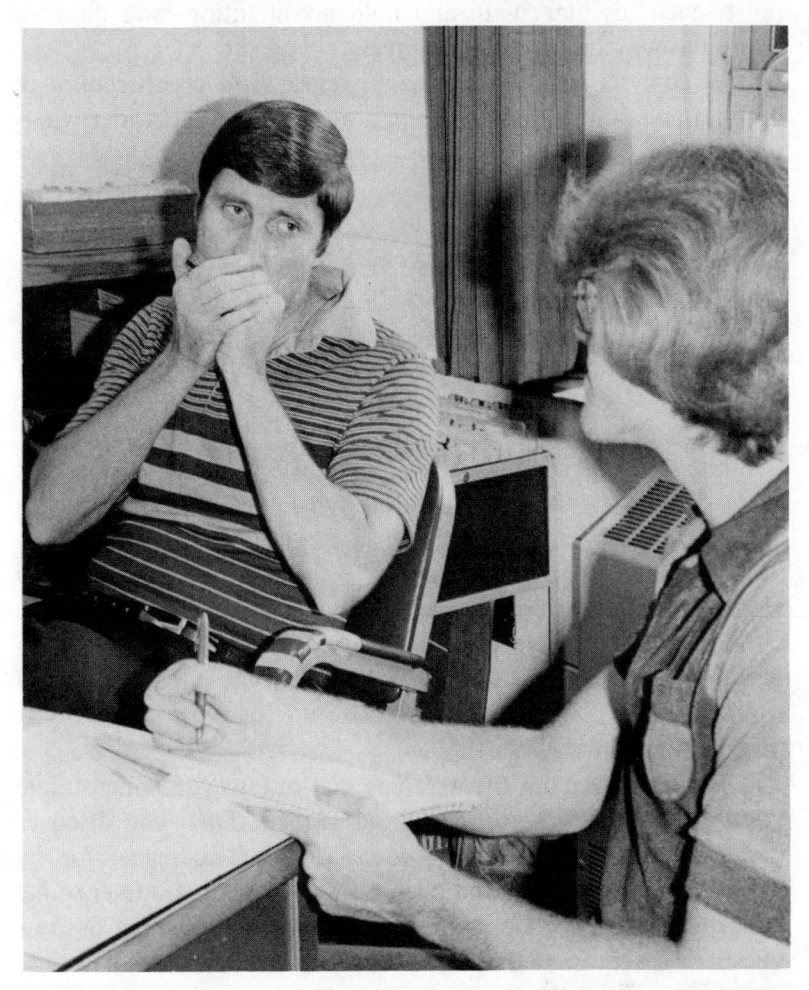

Interviews with teachers frequently lead to sidebar stories. Who would have dreamed that this biology teacher, being interviewed about the science fair, is a top contender in harmonica playing in folk festivals?

and that the questions are relevant and not carelessly thrown together.

A third secret:

A reporter can discover some helpful suggestions by noting how a good salesman works. For example, a salesman knows that he must start out with the buyer's point of view, that he must reach his man, gain and hold his attention, and direct it along the way he wants it to travel.

The application: to secure an interviewee's co-operation, to get him to talk, to lead him to talk about what the reader wants to know.

Situations Vary, Too

Because no two people are alike, no two interviewing situations will be alike. The reporter must be resourceful, adaptable, quick, ready. Generally interviews go much as you expect, especially if you are well prepared so you have plenty of questions and plenty of confidence. However, there are exceptions.

For example:

Suppose you encounter an individual who is very reluctant to talk, who does not respond to your efforts to conduct a friendly conversation. Sad fact: There is no solution for the first time this happens to you. However, from then on, you have only yourself to blame if you are not prepared for this possibility.

Solution: Have plenty of questions ready, well-planned questions, so if he merely says "yes" and "no" you have a fairly good story anyway.

Another example:

The interviewee has the welcome mat out, so you congratulate yourself that all will go to your advantage. Then you discover that he apparently considers you a captive audience, for he usurps the conversation and cheerfully fills the appointment time with only what he chooses to say. You leave with none of your questions asked.

Solution: To make the best of this, you can only select a story idea from what he has said. When you discover this is happening, as it may sometimes, make the most of it. Generally you can come up with some unifying thought, for his talk is likely to follow some main idea.

Critical Moments

Not only student reporters have their critical moments in interviewing. In a book entitled *We Cover the World,* fifteen correspondents for the Associated Press tell some of their experiences in meeting famous leaders around the world.

Among these, Eugene Lyons tells of his visit with the Shah of Persia. After elaborate arrangements had been worked out, it was agreed that Lyons would ask five prescribed questions to which the Shah would make five prescribed answers.

Upon his arrival at the palace, Lyons discovered the Shah to be friendly, shaking hands and offering him a chair by the fireplace. The questions were duly asked and answered in five minutes and Lyons expected to be dismissed.

"However," he said, "the Shah seemed to enjoy the novelty of having a reporter in and smiled invitingly for me to shoot some more questions.

"It was there, in the Shah's workroom, that I made a solemn vow. Never again, I pledged in my secret mind, would I come into the presence of the great of this world without scores of questions carefully prepared in advance for an hour or two of interview—even though the arrangements called for only a few minutes of it.

"Once before, I had been caught off guard. I had faced Stalin for what was understood to be a two-minute conference—just long enough to enable me to testify that the reports of his 'assassination' were 'exaggerated.'

"At the end of two minutes I found that Stalin was in no hurry, and there I was without a program of interrogation. I remained in Stalin's office nearly two hours and forever after would reproach myself for having failed in the excitement of the thing to ask significant questions.

"And here I was, facing another dictator, with a crackling fire in the grate, oodles of time ahead—and no questions prepared beyond a dull, pre-arranged routine."

Chapter XII

WATCHING FOR NEW ANGLES

A reporter setting out for an interview never knows what may be in store for him.

His assignment may be routine, perhaps to see the chairman of the math department about the national mathematics test to be given in the forthcoming weeks. Or the assignment may be unusual: to interview the artist's model who is unexpectedly visiting the art department to discuss modeling with the painting class.

The enthusiastic reporter goes prepared for both stories. He also goes fully aware that something unexpected may appear.

He knows that only alertness will help him in these moments. His only preparation for these "bonanzas" can be the knowledge that they may be there. This in itself is a help, feeble though it may seem.

Let us repeat here that interviewing is the basis for two kinds of stories:

(1) The news story, such as the commencement program, or the choral concert, or the testing schedule, or the Key Club convention, or the summer school schedule. That is, merely visiting sources of information for facts about what is going on.

(2) The feature story. This term covers a wide variety of stories that come from information gained in visiting with the interviewee. Many of these are by-line stories and as such include the interviewer's reaction, something of the setting, the personality of the interviewee, and the like. These are the stories where the author displays his creative imagination, subject, of course, to the limitations imposed by the restraints of journalistic writing.

Watching for New Angles

In both the routine and unusual assignments, new angles may turn up.

For example:

In visiting with the math teacher, you note that she has on

When you put a question to an interviewee, you expect an answer. Are you prepared to listen with your complete attention? The interviewee will be much more likely to talk freely if he finds that you are sincerely interested in what he has to say.

her desk a small computer that you have not seen on your previous visits there. You inquire about this after you get the information for the math test and discover that your school has been named one of four in the state for a pilot program in the use of computers in the classroom. So you have another story—a *new* news story.

And then she says, "This is expected to aid in the motivation of students who become discouraged and disinterested, perhaps even lead to a decrease in the dropout rate."

You note her enthusiasm here and make an appointment for another interview—this time to discuss with her the way she proposes to use the computer with her "retarded" class.

Did we say this was a *routine* assignment?

Now back to the artist's model:

This model was an elderly man, and the student reporter who was to have the unexpected opportunity to interview him had a newspaper clipping about him, nothing else. No background information. All he could do was to read up on models and modeling in general and then dash over to the art department.

He tried to make some plans as he went, assuming that his story would cover the visit and perhaps give something of the model's interesting experiences with artists, or perhaps something concerning modeling as a career.

The assumptions were correct. Friendly and pleasant, the model was happy to tell about his experiences with several of the world's famous artists.

But somewhere in the first few minutes of the conversation, he dropped a comment that he had been born into a circus family.

This fired the reporter's imagination, so he asked a question, and that led to others. He wrote two stories, the one assigned and one about how the circus family managed to educate their children while on the road, with the grandmother teaching the lessons between rehearsals for their acts.

Another example:

You decide to do a story about having portraits made for the yearbook, so you set up an appointment with the photographer and go prepared to talk about what students should know about how to "help" the photographer get a good picture.

The photographer is friendly. "Glad you're interested in running the story," he observed. "I was just thinking about the same thing day before yesterday while flying in from Alaska."

Alaska! Flying in . . . Of course you do the story on yearbook photos. And you do another story about the photographer-pilot. This one turns out to be a thriller, with the hero sitting there calmly across the table from you.

Creative Listening

A kind of *creative listening* begins when you first discover that no assignment is merely routine.

It may be called routine, but where there are people engaged in activities, there is nothing to be taken for granted.

Your enthusiasm can detect this, your enthusiasm coupled with a sincere interest in people. And your enthusiasm can help you do every story to the best of your ability. If you learn to do the small stories well, you will be ready for the big ones when they come.

If you train yourself to look for stories, especially by being on the alert for new angles, you will eventually be able to detect the big ones in the making.

Chapter XIII

*NOTING ADDED DETAILS OF
SETTING, PERSONALITY*

An interview is actually a little play. It has characters, setting, action.

Most of us are so concerned with the action that we overlook the importance of the setting and of the characters as personalities.

If you are writing a feature story based on the interview, everything about the occasion is important. Details can be very significant. Whether you include every item in your story or not, you must be aware of the "total picture" for the "total story."

You as a writer have the power of selectivity, choosing what you want to include in the finished piece—but this is entirely different from incomplete coverage.

The reader's curiosity will include details of the "total picture," for he will visualize as he reads. This means that you must create the picture of the interview for the reader.

He will want to see, feel, hear, taste, smell. Everything you put into this story of the interview is going to help give the reader the total impression.

Red Smith, sports columnist, says, "Get where the cabbage is cooking and catch the scents!"

Ideas for Color

Suggestion: Try taking "mental" pictures for the reader as you conduct the interview.

Mary Knight, a foreign correspondent for the Associated Press, well-known for colorful, vivid copy, offers this comment:

"I never could take pictures, with a camera, that looked like anything when they were developed," she said. "But anything I

Noting Added Details of Setting, Personality

The story is about the "Senior of the Month," so the enterprising reporter seeks to learn more about his interests and out-of-school activities.

can see and click with my own mental shutters makes a good print that stays with me."

Another suggestion:

If, in addition to improving your interviewing skills, you wish to write stories that will have special reader appeal, note this:

When two persons come face to face in an interview, they communicate by words—but the words are supplemented by other means of communication.

Try this the next time you are engaged in an interview. Have a list of the following items and check them off, mentally, as the conversation progresses:

(1) Facial expression, (2) general behavior, (3) posture, (4) gestures, (5) glint of the eye, (6) qualities of voice, (7) inflection.

Study the interviewee as you would a character on the stage. What is his general appearance? What is he wearing? Does he have any characteristic expressions or mannerisms? Are there any articles that would help characterize him—as a big cigar, loud tie, heavy signet ring—or, if a woman, a flower in her hair, red high-heeled sandals, a jeweled case for sunglasses?

The following examples show how this feeling for color is woven into the story. The first two are by professional writers, the others by students:

> Princess Grace, still as beauteous as the movie star she was ten years ago, glanced out the window before settling into a chair in the cool, aquamarine study of her palace.
>
> Below was a cobblestone courtyard, vacant except for a sentinel and a gleaming black and red 17th-century carriage, long minus its six white horses.
>
> And beyond the high walls of the medieval castle, with its porticos and square towers, were winding roads, tumbling stone fences, flat, pink-tiled houses, lush, flowering foliage, soaring cliffs and cottony clouds. Cascading to the crystal blue sea were 380 acres of this rocky enclave on the Côte d'Azur—the small, charmingly anachronistic world which is Monaco.

Noting Added Details of Setting, Personality

"It's really hard to believe," she sighed.

The former Grace Kelly, now Her Serene Highness, was not referring to the fantasy before her, no, nor to . . .

(From the Associated Press)

Like most test pilots, big Jack Reeder of NASA's Langley Research Center, in Hampton, Va., lets his hands do most of his talking: They pitch, roll, yaw, and sideslip like those of a symphony conductor.

One day last week, Mr. Reeder gently lifted his right hand from a conference table, shot it forward, slowed to a hover, then landed it vertically with a gentle slap on the burnished table top.

Mr. Reeder was describing what it's like to fly the British-made Hawker P-1127, one of the most advanced V-STOL (vertical-short take-off and landing) aircraft in the world . . .

(From the *National Observer*)

Roger Williams, whose talented fingers turned "Autumn Leaves" into a piano favorite, made a quiet entrance without the familiar ovation.

Actually, the applause was small because the stage was the lobby of a Columbus hotel, and the audience consisted of four amateur journalists seeking an interview with the musical celebrity . . .

(From the *Redbird,* Loudonville, Ohio)

Donning overcoat and hat, Mr. C. R. Turner braved the bitter cold of a winter night to demonstrate his latest hobby to an enthusiastic reporter.

With telescope in hand, Mr. Turner stepped into the night air and promptly began to talk.

"That's Jupiter right up there. It's the brightest object in the sky right now," he observed, while carefully placing the telescope in its stand.

Taking careful aim, he zeroed in on the planet, and after focusing it, he grumbled, "It's not too plain tonight . . . lots of glare . . . That's caused by . . ."

(From *Hope Hi-lights,* Hope, Arkansas)

Gold and black parachutes, smoke streamers and the "oh's" and "ah's" of the crowd filled the air as the Golden Knights showed Fort Smith this afternoon why they are the nation's champion parachute team.

Excitement reigned as the parachutists began to jump, and cries of "Why doesn't he open the parachute?" filled the air. People began to be worried, but I wasn't. I knew the exact moment the parachute would open and, with a smug smile, told the people around me. I had had an exclusive press interview with the master of ceremonies of the show here at the airport just before the exhibition began.

Sgt. Doug Colbert explained about the air spectacular, sponsored by the local United Fund Committee, from an improvised platform at the airport.

He was the perfect image of a parachutist, tall, slim, bronze, blue-eyed, and of course sporting a crew cut. He wasn't jumping, he said, because of a slight injury . . .

(From the *Grizzly,* Fort Smith, Arkansas)

Writer Is Painter

In certain kinds of interview stories, the writer has the same problem as the landscape painter. He must give depth, color and significance to his work in swift, sure strokes.

Chapter XIV

SUMMARY CHECKLIST

In an effort to help the beginner keep in mind the many suggestions made in reference to interviewing, the following checklist has been compiled. It combines lists of points-to-remember offered by professional journalists, psychologists, personnel specialists, teachers, and students.

Many common pitfalls can be avoided if you carefully go over this list. Every interview, including your very first, can be successful if you keep these points before you.

Eventually they will form a pattern of procedure that will underlie all your efforts. If you work at them consciously, you will find that soon you will be guided by them subconsciously.

(1) Decide just what you want to accomplish.

(2) Allow time enough.

(3) Plan the interview carefully so as to adapt it to *its* special purpose. Isolate your central idea. Plan relevant questions.

(4) Study the background thoroughly.

(5) Take care to think through your purpose and formulate the questions in such a way that the interviewee can respond fully.

(6) Word your questions precisely so they are easily understood.

(7) Make sure that the interviewee understands exactly what your purpose is and exactly what each of your questions is.

(8) Listen carefully and consider the interviewee's answers in order to make certain that you understand him correctly and interpret his meaning.

(9) Open the interview with something of real interest to the interviewee and then let him talk. Your statements should stimulate his ideas.

(10) Be at ease yourself. Help the interviewee feel at ease.

(11) Establish pleasant associations.

(12) Gain and deserve the interviewee's confidence. The only ideal relationship for interviewing is mutual confidence.

(13) Practice taking the interviewee's point of view. Try to imagine what he will think of you, of your approach, of your vocabulary, of your story idea.

(14) Take time and care to record his answers accurately.

(15) But do not dawdle.

(16) Study all the answers and select significant points.

(17) Avoid trying to outwit the interviewee. He may retaliate by trying to outwit you, and succeed. This can lead to error, misunderstanding, misinterpretation, even wrong information.

(18) Let the interviewee tell his story, then help him supplement it.

(19) Keep on the subject.

(20) Keep the important questions in mind until adequate information is obtained on each. Then as soon as one question is fully answered, dismiss it so you can concentrate on the next one.

(21) Keep control of the interview.

(22) Give the interviewee opportunity to qualify his answers.

(23) Check answers whenever possible.

(24) Practice separating facts from inferences. Distinguish between (a) observed facts, (b) statements made by an interviewee, and (c) inferences from (a) and (b).

(25) If he gives you percentages, translate them into figures at once.

(26) Be on the alert constantly for errors.

(27) Do not assume that all persons interviewed on a single subject will agree.

(28) Get *all* the facts.

(29) Check results statistically against reliable criteria.

(30) Be alert for additional information, new angles.

(31) Be sure to express your appreciation.

(32) Secure a confirmatory written note of approval from the

Summary Checklist

interviewee if he is reluctant to have this information used with his name in the school paper. Do not print in school papers items given you in confidence or in "personal conversation" unless you have this approval, written. If you are in doubt about what to print, consult the statement of policy observed by your school paper.

(33) Be very careful about information given you in confidence. As a beginning reporter, you would do well to avoid listening to confidential items. You must not betray confidences.

(34) Be very careful not to print anything that would be

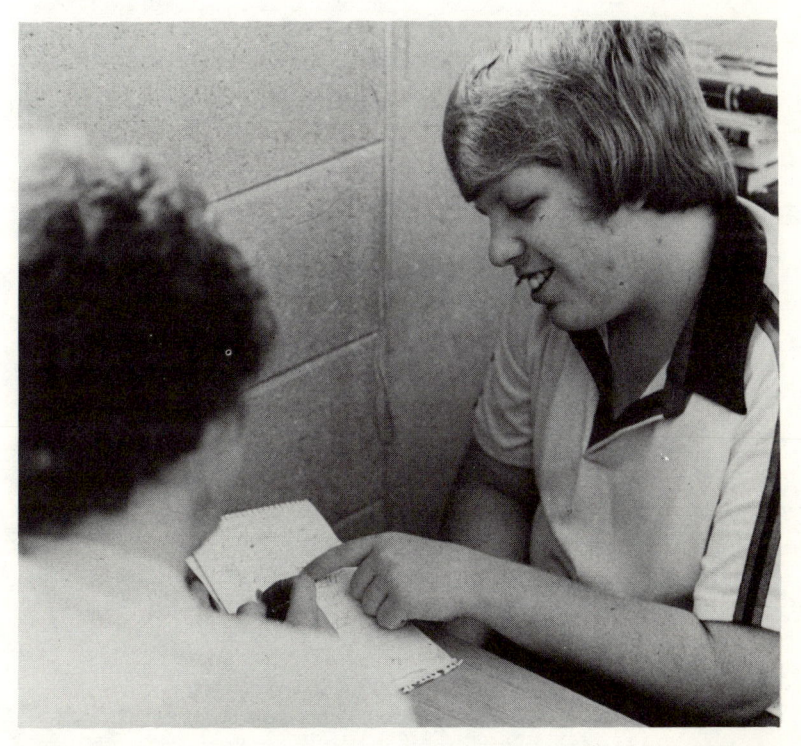

At the interview, quoted material must be checked especially carefully. The reporter re-reads his notes with the interviewee, making sure that his information is correct.

embarrassing to the interviewee. Professional reporters are involved in many kinds of stories—and they know what they are doing. But you, as a beginner, should learn first and "expose" later.

Chapter XV

TAKING NOTES

Every journalist, even the newest beginner, has to decide about taking notes.

But it's not a matter of whether to take notes or not to take notes.

The question is: What is the best way *for me* to take notes? Best, in this sense, means most effective, simplest, least conspicuous.

Even the most experienced reporters do not rely on their memory. They take notes carefully, fully—and written so they can read them later.

If they seem to be jotting down only a word here and there, it is because they have trained themselves over a period of time to listen with great concentration and then choose a few phrases that will capture the entire meaning for them when they get to a typewriter.

Even the most experienced writers hurry to the typewriter, for they know that the sooner you can transcribe your notes into full flowing sentences, the better.

No matter how much concentration you devote to taking notes and trying to impress the facts on your mind, time has a way of sweeping your memory clean. The longer you wait to transcribe your notes, the harder it will be to produce a complete, well-rounded account, rich with depth and color.

Notebook-Pencil Duo

From scraps of the grocery list to expensive tape recorders, reporters rely on some way to get the facts down so they can recall them later and reconstruct the meaning behind them.

But by far the most common articles used are the old friends of the student, the notebook and the pencil.

Ernie Deane, of the *Arkansas Gazette,* is typical of the professional man who has learned the importance of proficiency.

"I use a small notebook," he says. "It is easy to slip into your pocket, is easy to handle, and is inconspicuous."

This matter of being inconspicuous is worth considering, for some interviewees seem to grow shy in front of a large notebook, especially if the reporter labors over getting the ideas down on paper.

For this reason, being inconspicuous, many reporters prefer a short pencil. And they prefer a pencil to a pen in the first place, because quick erasing is possible.

However, pencils can sometimes cause problems. Penciled notes can be easily blurred or effaced, and eventually the words seem to fade into the paper.

Ink, or ballpoint, on the other hand, makes a permanent mark that is still legible for a long time later.

As a beginner, you won't think much about keeping notes and looking ahead to perhaps using them later. But here, too, you will be wise to consider what the professional writers do.

"I always keep my notes," Deane says. "Then later I look them over—to discover sometimes that what I *didn't use* at the time seems to have more value than what I *did use.* And often this leads to another story."

The editor in one of the large publishing houses in New York says that one reporter he worked with had more than a hundred pages of typewritten notes for a story that ran four pages in print.

Think as You Go

If you have prepared well in advance so you have your story line firmly in mind (and remember, it is best to write this as a complete sentence-summary in order to force yourself to "think unified")—and if you have sought background information diligently—and if you have your questions properly framed and in the correct order—then you will probably get through your interview with your notes in a well-organized pattern.

As you think back over your visit with the interviewee, you try to capture something outstanding about the experience and phrase this for your lead.

The remainder of the story usually then falls into place rather naturally.

This is no accident. This is your reward for having done your work well.

Taking notes. Sounds tedious, but one of the first lessons a young journalist should learn—and a practice he should always follow—is to take complete notes in legible form. "Gee, I can't read my notes" may sound amusing, but poor notes can spell disaster for a well-planned story.

It is the result of your having schooled yourself to follow certain techniques that have been suggested as effective.

Is Shorthand Necessary?
Should you learn shorthand?
This is a question everyone must answer for himself. Many reporters take a formal shorthand course in school, others devise a kind of quickie-writing.
You have a choice, but the point is this:
(1) Your system must be speedy, for in interviewing, you must not delay the conversation. A laboring pencil will always interrupt the speaker's train of thought.
(2) It must be effective. That is, you must be able to get down all the information you are going to need later—and get it down so you can read it when you want to.
Notes that are not usable are a complete loss and of course an inexcusable waste of time.

Checking as You Go
Your notes must be accurate.
Should you ask the interviewee to spell names that are not familiar to you? Yes.
Should you ask for sources for statistics and the like, about which the reader will wonder? Yes.
Should you stop to ask the interviewee if you have his meaning down correctly? Yes.
If you are serious about your questions and obviously interested in getting complete and correct answers, you will gain his condence and respect.

To Summarize:
Notes are not complete transcriptions of all that is said at the interview. They are thoughtfully selected words or phrases that are key words which will help you reconstruct the pattern of the interview later as you write the story.

PART FOUR

Writing the Story

Chapter XVI

*STUDY YOUR NOTES,
SEEK FRESH APPROACH*

Time, like the weather, is frequently mentioned in conversation—neither is generally taken very seriously.

To the reporter, however, time is a meaningful reality, a consideration in every story. Time, in newspaperdom, means deadlines.

That means *do it now*.

Begin at Once

The successful interviewer writes his story as soon as possible after he leaves the interviewee. If you want to become a successful interviewer, follow his example.

Immediately after the interview, if you can possibly do so, go over your notes. If you cannot find a few minutes to do this at once, then make every effort to get back to the notes as soon as possible.

Sometimes the problem is not a few minutes of time immediately, it's a quiet place to think. Actually, this can be solved better than a lack of time.

Solution: Simply get out your imaginary earplugs and deliberately concentrate on your story—in spite of distractions that may compete for your attention. This requires will power, you say? Of course it does.

98   Writing the Story

Getting off to a quiet place and going over your notes as soon as possible means that you can capture more of the mood of the interview than if you wait. The shorter the interval between the time you take notes and the time you look at them, the "warmer" your story will be.

There are several reasons for going over your notes as soon as possible after you leave the interviewee:

(1) This gives you an opportunity to go back over the conversation and fix it all in your mind by this deliberate repetition.

(2) It gives you an opportunity to recall consciously the details of setting, characteristics of the interviewee, and the like.

(3) It shows up any incomplete notes, any omissions of importance.

(4) It gives you a chance to look for inconsistencies, anything questionable. Sometimes you can catch errors this way and return at once to the interviewee—as for instance, in seeking facts about a play cast.

(5) It affords time for your imagination to add to the words you jotted down, so the notes are fuller in meaning when you get to the actual writing.

(6) It gives you an opportunity to add words you didn't have time to put down during the actual interview.

Write Immediately

Warning: The longer you let your notes lie unreviewed, the less they will mean to you. Whether you can write the story at once or not, *do read your notes and fill in as necessary,* so you can fix as much of the interview in your mind as possible.

Your notes will be much like a balloon, inflated and full of meaning to you when you leave the interview. However, just as a balloon begins to lose air, so your notes will lose fullness and meaning. Eventually the balloon is only a deflated reminder of what has been—and so with your notes.

Similarly, the sooner you can get to your typewriter, the better. Your enthusiasm, your "total view" of the story, your feeling for detail will be keener at first.

The only way to capture this is to get it into words at once. "Write before your notes get cold" is old advice, but still good.

Can you pump brightness into a forgotten idea? No.

Can you put life and sparkle into a wilted emotion? No.

Can you write a fresh, original story from neglected notes? No.

Keeping Your Notes

Beginning journalists have few interviews so important that they will want to keep their notes over a long period of time.

You never know, however, for once you enter the world of journalism and become an enthusiastic journalist, "thinking journalism" all the time, you will discover that you meet many interesting people, some of them even world famous. If you're quick and ready to take advantage of any unexpected opportunity, you may get an interview that will compete with the story the "big boys" do. Later, perhaps, these same notes will serve as background for another story opportunity.

Also, as long as you are in high school, you can use these notes for theme ideas.

Professional writers keep their notes so they can refer to them later if they want to. Sometimes this is a long, long time later. For example, C. F. Byrns, of the *Southwest American,* in writing a series of articles about the Arkansas River development program, referred to interviews with certain members of the senate two decades earlier, all carefully dated and filed in his notebooks.

A writer's notebook is one of his most prized possessions. Incidentally, he uses that term "notebook" loosely.

One of the faculty members at Columbia University tells this story for the truth:

"One of my young reporter friends who had been drafted was worrying about what to do with his things while he was in service, especially his notebooks," the professor said.

"Well, I could understand that, so I said, 'Don't worry about them. I'll keep them at my apartment for you while you're in service.'

"When the notebooks arrived, there were three trunks full of them!"

Reading Creatively

Once you have gone over your notes to see what you have jotted down as a record of the interview, you begin to look for new angles.

Why? Because the new angle is what gives your story freshness and originality—and because it often gives you an idea for a sidebar story, or possibly a tip for another interview or a sequel.

This play of *creative imagination* helps you give your story fullness and depth. It is this "creative" part of your writing that pleases your reader.

This creative imagination does not mean dreaming up weird ideas or distorting or extending the facts you have gained.

It means that your mind is actively engaged in seeking out what is most interesting so you can tell your reader about it. This may be drama, human interest, humor, conflict, unusualness—any of these qualities that are universally appealing.

For example:

A reporter was covering a tragedy that occurred on a mountain climbing expedition not long ago in Colorado. In asking questions, he learned that the youth who lost his life was a college student who was leading the expedition as a last-minute substitute for the regular guide for such parties.

As the reporter pondered his notes, he decided upon this as his lead idea. Then he recalled a comment that he had noted, that the victim had packed hastily in order not to delay the starting time and had failed to put in adequate clothing to protect him from an extended siege of freezing temperature. It was not the fall that was fatal—he froze to death, a result of his consideration for others and his concern that they not be disappointed or delayed.

This was the lead idea the reporter used. It was a result of his *creative reading* of his notes.

Chapter XVII

SUMMARIZE YOUR INFORMATION

To *be unified* you must *think unified*.

Unity is one of the essentials in writing. It is basic to complete understanding. No story has impact without unity.

No matter what kind of piece you are doing, it must "hang together."

There are many devices and techniques for achieving unity, but the best one is the simplest—merely to think unified.

If you have a story idea to begin with, carefully worked out, and if you are well prepared, then your story will almost write itself. Not because you are some kind of miracle worker, but because all your thinking was directed to your main idea and that else which was relevant.

Condensed Condensation

To summarize is not easy. It requires an active engagement with your mind.

You begin by condensing your information as much as possible. Then you condense your condensation. And then you try to write a headline for your condensation.

The headline is a kind of test. If you can come up with a satisfactory headline, then you can be reasonably sure that you have summarized well. If you are not able to phrase a satisfactory headline, then something is wrong somewhere.

Repeat: This writing of the headline is a good test.

By summarizing we mean phrasing the basic idea of the story in one complete sentence, if the story is reasonably short. If the story is long, then you will need more than one sentence for summary.

Questions Bring Answers

Your original story line and your summary will be identical in some cases, but not often.

Generally you will gain enough additional and unexpected

Why sit and stare at your outline, trying to decide which ideas are more important than others? Write each idea on a card, then arrange them in order of descending importance. Having each on a separate card means that you can shift them about to be sure that you have the most important ones first. You can even pretend that you are the printer and cut the paragraphs one at a time to decide which you would be most willing to omit if necessary.

information in your interview to cause alterations, or at least additions, to your original story line.

For example:

You go to interview the coach about the physical fitness program in the boys' physical education classes. You discover that a number of interclass tournaments are now in progress as a test of various skills.

You interview the coach about off-season activities in the athletic department and find that everything now revolves around an unexpected turn, re-sodding of the football field.

The point here:

Although you go to the interview with a carefully worked out story line and questions planned in accordance with what you expect the story to be, you usually discover information that alters your original idea.

In simple news stories, for which you are seeking facts about events or situations, this is not of great consequence.

When, however, your interview is to be the basis for what we call an interview story, then this alteration of your original story line is significant. And new angles and sidebar stories are always to be watched for.

Examples of summaries:

(1) Congressman Thomas D. Sutton today said that he thinks student council work is invaluable in training young people for active participation as adults in democratic procedures. He cited as examples . . .

(2) Central's biology instructor recommends horticulture for a most pleasant kind of "general therapy." The pressures of life today, he said, can be eased by . . .

(3) The senior council has chosen a musical melodrama to give a new look to an old tradition on this year's Senior Day. Complete with music, moustaches, and maidens in distress, the . . .

(4) Next September will bring an increase of 400 in enrollment to a building already filled to capacity and a faculty

limited by a budget now strained to meet the needs of summer school.

The Word Is 'Work'

In every discussion of writing, the word *work* comes up frequently. (It has been observed that the Five W's of journalism are Work, Work, Work, Work and Work.)

"Work" here means putting your mind into action. It means pushing your pencil, punching your typewriter keys. It does not mean listening to the radio while you are searching for an idea out in the wild blue yonder. It means concentrating your energies, both mental and physical, on trying to get down on paper something that satisfies you. It means trying, rejecting, trying again.

Secret of 'Genius'

Great achievement, it has been said, demands giving of life itself.

Noah Webster spent 36 years on the *American Dictionary of the English Language.* George Bancroft devoted 26 years to the writing of the *History of the United States,* Vergil was 12 years doing the *Aeneid.* Edward Gibbon worked 20 years on the *Decline and Fall of the Roman Empire* and rewrote his autobiography nine times.

Alexander Hamilton spoke for many when he wrote these words:

"Men give me credit for genius. All the genius I have lies in just this: when I have a subject in hand, I study it profoundly. Day and night it is before me. I explore it in all its bearings. My mind becomes pervaded with it.

"Then the effort I make the people are pleased to call the fruit of genius; it is the fruit of *labor* and *thought.*"

Chapter XVIII

ORGANIZE AND OUTLINE

"First think, then speak."

This old proverb could well be reworded for beginning journalists thus: "First think, then write."

Organize your ideas, outline.

That's the best advice when it comes to the actual writing of your story. Every teacher, every professional writer believes this. It's only *the way they say it* that varies.

Two Extreme Views

Some writers say they work best with a detailed outline, with all the subdivisions carefully filled in. What they really mean is that before they ever start writing, they think their story through very carefully.

They make sure that all the related parts are worked in just right. They check to see that balance, proportion and relationships are all considered.

Their outline is a record of all this thinking so they can sit down and run through the story, knowing in advance that it is unified and complete.

The opposite extreme is the writer who says that he never uses an outline, he merely writes the story as the parts seem to fall in place.

This is where the beginner is misled. He assumes that because this writer uses no written outline, he has done no pre-planning and thinking through his story.

Generally such a writer has the story well in mind and could dash off a complete and unified outline in a hurry if he needed to do so.

Organize and Outline

Between these two extremes lie many variations of plans of organization.

In composing stories based on interviews, such detailed outlines are not generally necessary for beginners. Professional writers who are doing long stories where the material is involved and the treatment complex, use their judgment about how much written outline is helpful.

In no instance is such an outline required. *The writer outlines his material because he wants to do a better piece of work.* The

Check names, check facts, check figures—check, check, check. No work habit you can develop will be any more important than this ceaseless search for accuracy. To be inaccurate is inexcusable.

outline is a kind of insurance against omissions, lack of proper relationships and incompleteness of the whole story.

Three Main Parts

As a beginning writer doing fairly short stories, you can divide your material into three parts—the beginning, the middle and the end. Within each part, then, you can select items in the order of importance.

The *beginning* is your lead and the paragraphs following, including the items necessary to summarize the story for the reader.

The *middle* is the main body of information which you would want to be sure your reader had next.

The *end* includes both the additional facts which you consider interesting and relevant and also a closing section.

This closing section for a news story is that body of least important facts which you would want cut first. But in a feature story you have a planned conclusion. True, sometimes the printer has to cut this in order to fit the story onto the page— but you as a writer should complete your feature story with a suitable ending which "ties up the point of the lead."

That is, as has been said, "your story should make a 'round trip'—so that some reference to the lead is repeated at the end of the story to give the reader a feeling of completeness."

A Good Idea

A helpful way of deciding on which paragraphs should come first is suggested by William J. Good, of the University of Arkansas.

"Write each paragraph of your story on a card," he says. "Then lay these out on a table and arrange them in order of descending importance. Consider which you would be willing to cut first if the printer did not have space for the entire story.

"Continue this process of elimination until you are satisfied that your most important ideas are at the beginning and that all are arranged in order of interest to the reader."

Outlining for Impact

Why so much effort to organize your ideas and outline your thinking?

Because if your story does not have orderly arrangement, it makes no impact.

Unless you know exactly what points you want to make and exactly how you want these presented, the reader will not respond as you want him to.

Nothing is ever any clearer in the reader's mind than it is in the writer's mind. Only if you *know definitely* what you want to communicate to the reader can you expect him to know.

Perhaps the most imaginative of outlining techniques is suggested by William H. Stringer, of the *Christian Science Monitor*. His procedure is often mentioned to show how professional writers view the art of organization.

"I simply pass out new and interesting points as the story continues," he says. "The point about advance preparation is simply this: Consciously or unconsciously, any good writer will have in thought some outline of what he wants to say. Often the order of his story will be formulated while he searches for a 'lead'—decides what should be said first, what second, and so on."

Keep Reader Interested

As a writer with ideas to convey to others, keep this in mind:

Today's reader is hurried, many things clamor for his attention at all times—and so his glance at your story may be merely a passing glance. If so, then you want him to see as much as possible before he can turn his attention elsewhere.

But know this: He may be interested enough in that first glance to read another sentence—and perhaps another yet if you have done a good job.

Remember, if you keep him for the first sentence, he will read the second. If you can keep him for the third, he will read the fourth, and so on. He may even read the entire story. As a careful writer, enthusiastic about your subject, you want to be prepared for that possibility.

This understanding of the complete story and your role in organizing your ideas is called *"a sense of inner architecture"* by John Gunther in *Fragment of Autobiography: Fun of Writing the Inside Books.* "Nothing," he says, "can be more useful to a writer."

Chapter XIX

WORK OUT A LEAD

Fifteen editors of high school papers, attending a workshop at the University of Oklahoma, had made a visit to the nuclear reactor and were now drifting into the lab to compose a story based on their interview with the director in charge.

About a third of them went to typewriters and began pounding out their ideas. Some six or eight others sat down with pencils and paper, obviously composing, but with slow deliberation. The remainder of the group hunched over their notes, scribbling here and there in an effort to get the start of a story.

Differences in skill? Not necessarily.

Not all stories come equally easy for all writers at the same time. You can expect some stories to come more easily for you than others do.

Expect Differences
Sometimes you will dash to the typewriter and the story will almost write itself. At other times, you will feel that only with a pencil can you entice the words and sentences to the paper. They will come slowly, but you will have the feeling that they are falling into place and your story is taking shape.

Occasionally, no matter how much preparation you have put in and how much thought you have given, neither the typewriter nor the pencil will write your story—and then you must search your mind, struggle for ideas, scribble a few lines, discard—and try again.

The secret to success here is *keep on trying*. There is no miracle worker for you to summon. You must create your own miracles, if you expect any.

Writing the Story

Getting Started

Do you have trouble getting started? Do you find that sometimes nothing, absolutely nothing, seems to work out? Do you feel hopelessly blank?

If your answer here is "yes," then you have what we call "starter trouble" and "keeping-on-going trouble."

Solution:

(1) *Don't* let the typewriter sit there and stare at you.

(2) *Do* engage briefly in some activity that will break the freeze. Try eating an apple or a cookie, or pick up a book of quotations and thumb through a few interesting phrases, or even turn to a page in the dictionary and read definitions of words completely new to you.

To keep your fingers moving over the keys, begin typing your

If you have difficulty getting started, try this. Write: "I just saw (or heard) the most interesting thing. It went this way . . ." Then simply and fully tell what your notes cover. Somewhere in this recounting of your information, you will give yourself a beginning idea.

notes. If possible, type these from memory, but look at them if you need to. The point is that you must keep your fingers moving. If you're using a pencil, then keep pushing it, every second. Don't stop until you feel that your thoughts can take off by themselves.

Beginnings First

The logical place to start your story is at the beginning.

If you have searched for a new angle, have composed your summary sentence and have outlined your ideas, you are ready to work on your lead.

Probably at this point you already have what we call the *lead idea.* That is, you know how you want to begin.

Your only concern here is how to phrase this so it will be most effective and so it will lead the reader right into the body of your story. The *lead* is a carefully phrased expression of the *lead idea,* with consideration given to both meaning and sound.

Lead idea: Crime is increasing in the nation.

Lead: Every time the clock ticks off a minute and a half, there is a robbery, burglary, hold up, theft, or embezzlement somewhere in the United States.

Lead idea: This is an age of speed.

Lead: Man may have no idea where he is going, but wherever it is, he will soon be going there at speeds of upwards of 3,000 miles per hour.

Lead idea: Last week was a busy one in Washington.

Lead: Washington worked hard last week, grinding out history complete with footnotes.

A Matter of Sound

Frequently you will hear this: "I know what I want to say, but it *doesn't sound right!*"

This feeling is identified with rhythm in language, says Foster-Harris, of the University of Oklahoma. Suggestion: Try reading your lead aloud.

Although you may not know why you do so, you will begin

to rephrase in more rhythmic language and thus improve the sound. Once it sounds right to you, as you hear yourself say the words, you can continue.

Lead Idea Sufficient

If you cannot work out a lead to your satisfaction, do not fret.

Do this: Consider your lead idea carefully. Be certain that it covers exactly the idea you want to use for a beginning. Write this as your beginning and then follow with the body of the story, just as you would if you had completed the lead.

Later, when your story is finished, you can return to this and work on it as long as you can, or until it satisfies you. Many times the "right words" will flash into your mind as you are working on a part of the story. In this event, *stop the story and work on the lead at that moment.*

Ideas do not wait for you. Get them down in words immediately.

Suggestion:

In order to improve your ability in writing leads, make a collection of leads that please you. Clip these, or copy them, paste them on 3" × 5" cards, tag each one to show why you thought it good, and file for quick reference. Merely reading through them will refresh you if you feel dull and uninteresting.

The Five W's

For straight news stories the best beginning is still the well-known Five W Formula—who, what, when, where, why (and how).

These are the basic elements in which readers are interested. The *who* and the *what* are generally most important and so are usually mentioned first in the phrasing of the lead.

Since the first transmission of news by telegraph during the Civil War, this has been accepted as the quickest way to get the essence of the news to the reader. This kind of lead is called the straight summary lead.

Examples:

(1) Coach John R. Lane will be honored at a special luncheon meeting of the Kiwanis Club Thursday for his 20 years of service to the Grady High School Key Club, sponsored by Kiwanis.

The luncheon, to be at the Morton Hotel at 12 o'clock, will be attended by . . .

(2) In recognition of seniors in this area who have made outstanding academic records, KFSA radio beginning Monday will select daily some student from the local schools for a short interview.

(3) Steve Bradford, THS senior, has been named winner of the grand prize, a $50 savings bond, in the Crime Prevention Week poster contest sponsored in the city schools by the local Exchange Club.

Examples showing how the various W's are used effectively:

Who—when the person is more important than any other element:

Gayla Mhoon, NSHS junior, has been elected secretary for the district library convention to be held on this campus May 10.

What—when the event is most important:

Central's annual battle of titans takes place one week from tonight as the Key Club and the faculty meet in their annual benefit basketball tilt at 7:30 in Norris Gym.

When—when the time is especially significant:

Tomorrow begins the annual turnabout, sponsored by the student council, in which the girls ask the boys out and pay the bill, otherwise known at Hammond High as Twirp Week.

Where—when the place is of special interest:

Place—the back campus. Time—after school tomorrow. Props —pruning shears. Why? The Future Journalists of America are planning to trim the fast-growing shrubbery they planted last year by the east entrance.

Why—when explanation seems like a good *attention-getter:*

To guide seniors in choice of college, to determine shortcomings in scholastic progress and to aid in the awarding of scholarships, the Hall guidance department plans a series of various tests for HHS students this year.

How—when explanation is interesting:
Displaying their new "jet offense," the Northside Bruins romped to two impressive victories over conference foes this week in Grizzly Gym, defeating Jonesboro 59-41 Tuesday night and El Dorado 64-50 last night.

Feature-Summary

Many times one of the W's is much more interesting or important than the others. When this is true, you feature that W by placing it prominently in the summary, usually first, and by giving it more space.

This is called a *feature-summary lead*. Effective openings for this type of lead include striking statements, questions and quotations.

Examples:

(1) Does money speak louder than sentiment?

This is the question based on a current problem facing the student council, a problem that started more than a year ago. Debate continues over whether to sell the Spirit Truck or pay the cost of repairs and keep it because of its sentimental value to the school.

"The estimated cost of repairs exceeds what we now have in the budget for the truck," stated Bruce Sutton, SC president, yesterday in discussing . . .

(2) The new lights are up, the costumes are in order, sets have had their last stroke of paint, all the lines and dances are down pat.

Tonight is the final dress rehearsal for this year's musical, *South Pacific*.

Tomorrow night when the curtain rises at 8:15, the cast will face a sell-out crowd as the Rodgers and Hammerstein musical opens for the first of four performances in Norris Auditorium.

Variety in Leads

Your own judgment and your interest in what you have to write will determine how you phrase your lead. It is helpful, however, to know that certain openings not only are popular but usually fit in well. If you are having trouble getting started, you may get ideas from running over in your mind some of the favorite variations.

In school papers where there is much feature treatment of old news and where feature stories such as the interview story are especially popular, wide variety in leads is suitable.

Grammatical Structure

Seeking variety in grammatical structure often helps give freshness and originality to leads.

(1) Prepositional phrase:

In the anticipation of the approaching hot weather, final adjustments were recently completed on the new 15-ton air-conditioner unit installed in the band room.

(2) Participial phrase:

Celebrating their 75th anniversary, the Athenian Literary Society has planned a reception for past members, sponsors and faculty to be held Thursday at 7:30 p.m. in the school cafeteria.

(3) Introductory adverbial clause:

    (a) When the Tiger band steps out on the field at the first football game next September, fans will see a complete change in uniforms and marching format.

    (b) Because a machine started spitting lead at a Linotype operator last week, the print shop faces a $200 emergency expenditure for repairs.

(4) Infinitive:

To honor club presidents and sponsors, the Key Club will stage their 20th annual appreciation banquet Tuesday at 7 p.m. at the Mountain Inn.

Sentence Variety

Another kind of classification, by sentences, seeks to show additional variety.

(1) Simple statement:

Racing fever, in miniature form, has hit an all-time high in the Memphis area the past few months.

(2) Striking statement:
    (a) In 45 minutes this afternoon the Journalism Club marched through 240 million years of history at Stovall Museum.
    (b) Dan Johnson's general science classes are at it again.
        The clanking of wrenches in room 120 proves that another project is in progress to help students see how science influences their environment.

(3) Question:

What does the term "North Central accreditation" mean?

This question was asked when the State Evaluation Committee of the North Central Association of Colleges and Secondary Schools visited Southside High School this week, and it will be asked again when the committee visits Northside in 1967-'68 to re-evaluate this school.

(4) Quotation:

"One out of every 30 students attending Central will drop out before this school year is over, if the present rate continues," said Thomas Grace, principal, yesterday in addressing the Parent-Teacher Association Council.

(5) Narrative:

An air of electric excitement filled the auditorium. Defiance, determination and resolution were registered on many faces as the audience quietly filed in and took their seats.

The president of the student body stepped to the microphone.

The purpose: the perennial question of abolishing the House of Representatives, yes or no, once and for all . . .

(6) Novelty:
    (a) Lick . . . stick . . . lick . . . stick . . . lick . . . stick . . . sick . . . sick . . .
        This is the song of the savings stamp collector who toils many hours to fill books and redeem gifts splendidly advertised in the catalogue.

(b) Mud was here, mud was there, mud was everywhere—the homecoming royalty walked through it and the football team played in it.

(c) A bear is a bear is a bear . . . but at Northside this isn't always true.

The best-known bear-about-campus is really Barry Coplin, Northside senior, clothed in the student council's genuine-imitation Grizzly bear costume.

Other Variations

Other suggestions for variety in leads include the following, a selection of four favorite openings from a group of many possibilities.

(1) Picture:

Dancing brown eyes, clipped black hair, polished toe nails, and a name of Patrice Mumselle all make for a beautiful pet and a profitable business.

This French poodle, boasting a pedigree . . .

(2) Punch:

The House has won again.

Voting on the perennial question of whether or not to abolish the House of Representatives, the student body for the fifth time in as many years . . .

(3) Allusion:

"Neither a borrower nor a lender be" certainly does not apply to the THS library, lender of 11,365 books and 110 different magazines.

(4) Contrast:

(a) It may be winter to the weatherman, but Amarillo thinclads know no season boundaries as they prepare for the approaching track schedule.

(b) Today in America there is a curious medical contrast: The patient seems fine. But the doctor is uneasy.

Forecasting the Story

As you study the leads of stories that appeal to you, you will observe that the effective writer has a way of forecasting the story in the opening words. This is actually more than a summary. It is a summary with a future look.

He not only knows exactly what he wants to say and thus is in complete control of his ideas, he also has a way with words. It is this that gives his lead a *plus quality*.

These "super leads" are often the very simplest in both idea and phrase.

For example, in covering astronaut John Glenn's flight, Frank McGee began his television report thus: The flight is over, but the story is not yet complete.

Sometimes leads are characterized by color, as these leads on Associated Press stories:

(1) Moscow today just about owns Cuba—lock, stock, barrel, and beard.

(2) Last night New York glowed with embellished brilliance, smelled of freshly cut spruce, and rang with cash registers and the bells of sidewalk Santas.

In identifying the characteristics of good leads, Lewis Jordan of the *New York Times,* says this: "The writers have told what their stories are about in simple, clear sentences. And there is sprightliness where it is appropriate."

Question of Length

How long should a lead be?

This is a frequent question. It stems from an understanding that in this visual-minded age the writer must gain the attention of the reader immediately.

The writer knows that if he can attract the reader to the first sentence, he may be able to capture his attention for one or, hopefully, more.

Opening sentences should be fairly short. They should be *attention getters*. This does not mean necessarily that they should be shocking statements or displays of weird punctuation.

Even a very short sentence will capture your attention. For example, the lead on a story about the return of the first war casualties from the European theater was simply two words: They're home.

As to length, a good rule is this: Try to keep your first sentence to twenty-five words or less. If your first sentence runs to more than this, it is wise to consider it carefully to see if you can rephrase it more effectively.

Frequently you can revise by dividing and using two sentences. Many writers now put the most important W's in the first sentence and then follow with the others in the next sentence or two.

Caution: Do not try to load your opening sentence with too many ideas strung together.

About Paragraphing

Special note: You do not paragraph a news or feature story the way you do a composition for your English teacher. A story in the newspaper must be broken up if it looks attractive. News and feature stories are not expository paragraphs built around a topic sentence.

Stories in newspapers follow a pattern of their own. This pattern calls for paragraphing the information so it can be read rapidly, comprehended easily.

Long Openings

As you work on your lead—and you are in the company of professional writers when you do this, for even the best labor over their leads in an effort to get the story off just right—you will eventually make a startling discovery.

You will find that a "lead" (defined as one sentence) and an opening are not necessarily the same.

For instance, especially in a long story, your sense of proportion will indicate that you need a longer opening than only a sentence or two.

And so you begin to use the term "lead" a little more thoughtfully. You realize that the opening of the story—which summarizes your total idea and forecasts something of the tone—is not measured in a given number of sentences but is rather the way you get your story moving.

The following entry in a recent Quill and Scroll contest shows how a long opening section seems suitable for a by-line piece that runs to some 20 column inches:

> Are you plagued by headaches, muscular pains and digestive trouble?
> Do you bite your nails, yell at people and get upset too easily?
> One dreary day when my answer to all these questions was "yes" and upon noticing that some of my fellow students seemed to be beset by these same problems, too, I decided that it was time for a counseling session with the school nurse, Miss Maryella Clayton.
> In a matter of minutes she diagnosed the trouble—tension.
> "Tension is a stress or strain on the nerves," said Miss Clayton. "It is caused by . . ."

Quick Checklist

Common errors among beginners can be avoided by following this checklist:

(1) Avoid beginning opening sentences with *a, an,* and *the,* unless absolutely necessary. (Obviously, you must use your judgment here. If the word *a, an,* or *the* is essential in the opening, then use it. The point is, that unless you watch and strive for variety, you are likely to have every story in the paper beginning with one of these.)

(2) Avoid beginning all leads with the same grammatical construction, as subject first, then predicate, or you will fall into a kind of subject-predicate monotony.

(3) Avoid beginning with a participle and then following with an auxiliary verb and a subject. The preferred form is the participle as a phrase and then a subject and a verb.

For example, avoid this: Reigning this week as the Royal Maids of Music are four girls from the mixed chorus and three from the band.

Better: Reigning this week as the Royal Maids of Music, four girls from the mixed chorus and three from the band were elected Monday by members of the choral and instrumental music departments for this traditional honor.

(4) After you have phrased your lead, check opening words of paragraphs in the story when you complete it to see that you do not begin several paragraphs with the same words.

(5) Read your lead aloud so you can listen for sounds that might not be pleasing. Occasionally, alliteration or near rhyme lends an unattractive element to your combination of words. This is likely to go unnoticed unless you look for it.

(6) Check to see that you have cited your authority if this authority is necessary in the story as you are writing it.

(7) Avoid the use of *according to* unless you mean *in accordance with*.

(8) Be sure that you have identified this authority properly.

(9) See that you have included all the necessary W's in your opening.

(10) Remember: *Never overestimate the knowledge of your reader. And never underestimate his intelligence.* That is, be mindful that he may not be at all familiar with the information about which you are writing. Also bear in mind that today's public is well educated.

Your friends may not want to admit it in this age when it is popular with teen-agers to play everything down—but the teenage audience is really discriminating. If you write like a young child, thinking they will be attracted by this, you are indulging yourself. Try writing *up* for them. This may surprise you more than it will your readers.

(11) Consider carefully the words you use. We talk about synonyms, but actually there are few synonyms in the language. For example, one student was writing about a *huge hunt*. This is not an adequate adjective. The word has to do with size rather than with extent. The hunt was *extensive*.

Make friends with the dictionary and the thesaurus. Learn to read for the right word, listen for the right word, choose the right word. The adequate word, the exact word, the specific word.

Sometimes the sound of the word is important in conveying your total meaning in the most pleasing way. Develop a "listening ear" for language. Take time to read aloud passages from your favorite authors.

(12) Scrutinize your copy for unnecessary words. Always be mindful of word economy. Condense wording so you will have more space for more ideas.

Words are precious. Use all you need—and no more than you need. Just as the exact word is an element in strong writing so is the exact phrase.

Chapter XX

FOLLOW WITH THE BODY OF THE STORY

"A well-planned story almost writes itself."

"Once the lead is worked out, the remainder of the story seems to fall into place."

Sounds encouraging, doesn't it? Encouraging enough that you want to believe it.

These statements are not wishful thinking. They are comments made by writers of long experience, writers who have discovered secrets of success.

Secrets? Yes. Simple secrets that are yours for the believing:

(1) For the well-planned story is one that you have worked on from the very beginning—from the first of your research on through the statement of your story line on to the actual interview and your complete notes on each question.

(2) For in working out the lead, you are actually organizing all the parts of your story, deciding how you shall lead off so the reader will follow you right on through the information you have for him. To repeat a favorite phrase: If you *think unified*, you will *be unified*.

If you have unity, you are likely to have impact.

One of the most delightful aspects of this is that as you work on a story that seems to "fall into place," you enjoy working on it—and in turn your enthusiasm for it is so obvious that the reader will be happy to follow you from one sentence to another.

This is not to say that this kind of writing necessarily "comes easy." Often it "comes hard." As one adviser-teacher observes, "There are times when you have to slug it out." But it comes with a satisfaction that is a deep-seated kind of pleasure. It glows through your words. And your reader responds.

News Story Form

A news story has a definite shape. This is based on the necessity of fitting a certain number of words into a given space.

The limitations of a page will not give. Therefore, the story must be fitted to the space. It must be written so that if necessary the ending can be cut. In many cases stories are cut severely, so that only the few opening paragraphs are run.

This means that the writer must be careful to include first that information that he considers most important.

This means that the make-up man is going to cut just as he needs to, with no thought for most important paragraphs deep in the story.

Inverted pyramid is the name we give to this shape of the news story.

As you write news stories, you will come to realize that this is a reasonable and helpful guide in organizing your material. All kinds of news stories—the fact story, the action story, the quote story—can be fitted to this form.

Feature Story Patterns

With feature stories, however, and this includes what we are calling the interview story, the simple news story form is not necessarily the best way to tell the story.

Frequently the feature story can be effectively concluded with some sort of tie-in with the opening. Frequently it is merely a step by step account. Occasionally, in an interview story, much of what you want to tell your reader is of equal importance.

Use your judgment about the form to follow.

If you feel that you must write a clincher line for the last paragraph to wrap up the account in grand style, do so. Then read it carefully and congratulate yourself one more time as to how good it is—*because* when the make-up man gets it, clincher or no clincher, he's going to cut if he needs to cut.

Every person who writes for publication must always be mindful that the story must be fitted to the page. The make-up man knows only one rule: cut to fit.

Therefore, as a beginning writer, you must train yourself to determine exactly how long your story should be—and then plan and write to that length.

Not until you are famous as a free lance writer whom all the editors are seeking can you write the story as you please and expect it to be printed in its entirety.

Indicating the Questions

In building an interview story, it is frequently possible to use your questions and the resulting answers as if they were building blocks. If these were well planned and if the answers followed as you expected, then your story will fall into place rather easily.

Although your questions and the subsequent answers did not go quite as you anticipated, they may still serve as units with which you can put the story together.

The problem here is how to bring in the questions so the story reads smoothly.

Various techniques are employed:

(1) The most common is the assumption of the question in the answer. For example, in the following story about tension among teen-agers, the questions simply elicited the answers that go into explaining about tension, causes, relief, and the like.

(2) A second popular way to indicate the question is merely to phrase the question as a question at the point where it logically fitted into the interview.

For example, the tension story progresses smoothly as it is built with the nurse's answers. However, when the emphasis is shifted to the matter of relief from tension, the writer breaks abruptly and stresses the point by using the question as a paragraph.

Note that two paragraphs answer this question. As the story is written, we assume that these are verbatim answers given by the nurse.

(3) A third technique is to summarize the question thus: When asked if he would ever leave the farm to retire in a city,

Mr. Miller answered, "No, there's nothing like seeing the sun go down behind the cattle barn after a hard day's work."

(4) A fourth technique, used occasionally, is a skillful repetition of the question by the interviewee. For example, an excerpt from an interview with a nationally known authority on yearbooks:

> Mr. Paschal smiled as he glanced around his office, indicating yearbooks cosily stacked on shelves, on the floor, on the chairs, on his desk.
> "Do I find that yearbook staffs are improving? Indeed, they are. In fact, every book here has been submitted for critical reading in the hope that . . .

(5) A fifth way to indicate the question is employed in long interviews where the emphasis is on the question-answer series rather than on a story about the interview.

For example, in the *National Observer* an interview on "Dilemmas and Distractions in Science's Changing Environment":

The introduction summarizes the subject thus:

> The current problems of science—from the conflict in the minds of scientists building hydrogen bombs to the lack of leisure for creative thinking—are discussed here by Dr. Hans Bethe, a prominent physicist and professor at Cornell University.
> The interview was conducted by Donald McDonald of Marquette University.
> Mr. McDonald: Dr. Bethe, what is the general condition of science and the scientific community in this country as compared to what it was when you came to the United States 27 years ago?
> Dr. Bethe: In some respects conditions have become better . . .

The article continues thus with questions and answers, nothing else. The questions are printed in italics.

Use of Quotes

In the usual news story, occasional quotes are included if the source of the information is important enough to quote or if certain items of information are his ideas or directly related to him.

Sometimes something interesting or unusual can be added to keep the story lively. If given as quote, this has reader appeal.

Quotes in a story make it look interesting. Caution: Do not quote nothingness.

For example, far too many beginners use far too many paragraphs like this: "We expect a large crowd and hope this will be a very successful program," John Sanders, president, stated.

Waste of time, words and space.

In interview stories, however, the thoughtful use of quotes adds *strength, color* and *variety* to your writing.

Often it also makes for *clarity,* since to quote the interviewee verbatim is to convey his meaning to the reader as the speaker conveyed it to you.

Caution: Be careful to run quoted material only a paragraph at a time. Successive paragraphs of quoted material are confusing for rapid reading.

It is much easier for the reader if you have one paragraph of quote and then one or more paragraphs of summary. Every other paragraph in quotes makes for both attractiveness and easy reading.

For example, following the lead on the story about tension among teen-agers, as discussed by the school nurse, the paragraphs were arranged thus:

"Tension is a stress or strain on the nerves," Miss Clayton said. "It is usually caused by worry, fear and pressure."

Most people are disturbed by some kind of problem. This includes students.

"Just as the businessman who is working for success is under pressure, so is a student," she explained. "The student working for good grades, for example, is under pressure either from his parents or the desire to go to college."

Not only is the student under pressure, he also worries about his grades and many times is afraid to receive his report card.

"These tensions can cause illness, both physical and emotional," she commented. "Many times the physical illness stems from the emotional."

When emotional tension is prolonged, the student may develop symptoms of a serious disease. Citing a magazine article, she told of a girl who never expressed her feelings but kept them bottled up, until they came out in the form of violent headaches.

"Many times such bottled up feelings are the cause of tension in teen-agers," she explained. "They are not given the opportunity for self-expression, either in classrooms or at home."

Even such things as a magazine article criticizing teens could cause emotional problems.

"This, once again, is another reason for tension," she said. "In society they feel a lack of approval, and in trying to gain a sense of security they face many anxieties, disappointments, successes or failures. Often they gain nothing but an inferiority complex."

What kind of relief is there for tension?

Various temporary reliefs are recognized, as smoking, chewing gum and tranquilizers. However, tranquilizers should not be taken except as prescribed by a doctor, Miss Clayton pointed out.

"Actually, you have to learn to live with tension, learn to play and relax," she said. "One of the main things in relieving tension is either to forget the unpleasant things or to learn to accept them and go about everyday tasks."

Showing Personality

Careful choice of quotes—based on careful taking of notes—can lend depth and color to an interview especially because the words a person speaks indicate a great deal about his personality.

They help describe him when you employ them in a story about him. They also hint at the situation.

For example, note the following answers to this question, "Do you think boys are smarter than girls?"

(1) Professor Timmons pondered this a moment. "Do I in-

terpret your question to refer solely to the quality of native intelligence?"

(2) The editor ground out his cigarette in the ash tray. "By golly, boys may be smarter, but when I need a good job done in a hurry with no fuss about it, I'd just as soon send one of the girls."

(3) Bub grinned. "You betcha life!"

(4) Susie Belle giggled and glanced over at Buster. "You mean could girls might re-e-e-e-ally be smarter than boys?"

(5) "Well, now—"

(6) "Actually, according to scores on national tests and in competitive examinations of various kinds, it does seem to appear that boys have an advantage over girls in certain areas and when you compensate for varying factors. However, . . ."

(7) Miss Baynes smiled above the heads of the little brood clustered around her desk. "How could anyone answer that question?"

(8) "Are you kiddin'!"

(9) The office manager shook his head. "That's a moot question."

(10) "Hoot, mon!"

(11) Auntie fluttered her eyelashes. "Oh, dear, yes. Yes, indeed. I really do."

Setting, Background

Since we are trying to give the reader as complete a picture as possible in the interview story, it is helpful if we add as much of the setting and background as are significant for our purpose.

For example:

(1) You are interviewing an architect who is especially well known for contemporary design. Your story would be more complete and stronger if you let the reader know that you are touring one of the interviewee's newest buildings.

As you quote him, you have a specific example to mention. This gives the reader something to see in his imagination as a background for the architect's comments about his work.

(2) You are interviewing a business executive who is an efficiency expert. You note that his office is extremely neat and that his desk is uncluttered. What he has to say about efficiency you can relate to the setting in which he operates.

(3) Or suppose you are interviewing another busy executive who is well known for accomplishing a great deal in several areas. You observe that his office is a very "busy" place. Everything he might ever want, it seems, is right at hand.

He smiles when he comments, "This may look disorganized, but I can find anything I want in just a minute. My only worry is that some 'efficient' secretary will come in some day and disorganize everything by trying to file them according to some system!"

(4) Suppose you are interviewing the shop instructor about the woodworking program. You note that bright colors are prominently used on and near the machinery. When you discover that the color is used to denote danger areas and to call attention to certain parts of the machines, you strengthen your story by telling about the setting.

Manner, Appearance

The interviewee's manner and appearance will also be of interest to your reader.

Does he smoke a pipe? Does he jam his hat down over his ears? Does he have a rollicking sense of humor? Does he wear a plaid jacket and bowtie? Carry a banjo under one arm? Have his nose in a book? Crumple the newspaper? Pound the desk when aroused about a subject? Peer at you thoughtfully when you pose a question? Is his voice even and low? Loud? Does he hunch his shoulders?

Suppose your interviewee is *une femme*. What is she wearing? What kind of perfume? Is she soft spoken or the crisp-voiced "executive" type? Is she wearing a corsage? waving an umbrella? toting a gun? Is her hobby tennis? Coin collecting? Antique cars?

Generally speaking, if your interviewee is a well-known person, as perhaps a television star, readers are actually more interested in how he, or she, appeared than in what was said.

Imaginary Camera

If you had a movie camera and expected to accompany your account with pictures, your mind would be busy during the interview selecting items of significance and interest.

The best substitute for a real camera is an *imaginary* one. As you conduct your interview, let your imaginary camera take very real pictures.

When you begin to compose your account of the interview, run back over this imaginary film in your mind and write as much of it as possible into your story.

This imaginary camera can be one of your biggest aids. Carry it with you wherever you go.

Strangely enough, we frequently see picture ideas before we realize that the same subject would be excellent for a story told in words.

PART FIVE

Developing Skills in Effective Expression

Chapter XXI

WRITING IS BOTH AN ART AND A CRAFT

Writing is an art in so far as it demands of the writer imagination, care for form, distinctiveness in style.

It is an art in so far as the writer himself must be a creative mind, intensely devoted to his ideas and determined to express those ideas in the most effective way his imagination can conceive.

Writing is a craft in so far as there are techniques, methods, rules, precepts for the beginner to learn and to try.

You Can Learn to Write

Because writing is a craft, every beginning journalist who really wants to learn a way with words can get a good start by listening to his teachers, by reading books on writing and by studying the work of those whom he admires and respects.

His progress from this starting point and his ultimate success are determined solely by his own enthusiasm and his industry.

Four Elements

There are four elements in good writing:
(1) The force of your idea.
(2) The clarity of your organization.
(3) The richness of your vocabulary.
(4) The smoothness of your sentences.

Fortunate is the young writer who learns early that the library is a treasure house. The reference section, especially, contains innumerable sources of information. The writer, even more than the reader, must feel at home among books.

If you keep these in mind, you can use them as a kind of mental checklist as you work on your copy.

Obviously, richness of vocabulary and smoothness of sentences are worthless unless you have a forceful idea. And even the strongest idea goes adrift in poor organization.

Good writing is related to good thinking.

In discussing qualities of effective expression, Henry Justin Smith, of the *Chicago Daily News,* points out that a good writer develops his personality as he works at writing. These include

(1) Being posted—knowledge of one's material, of one's atmosphere, of one's companions in the inexplicable procession of things.

(2) Fearlessness—without which knowledge cannot be had.

(3) Vigor—mental if not physical.

(4) Dash—or verve, as the French say—vivacity, liveliness.

(5) Sense of humor. If you do not have a sense of humor, try to acquire it by associating with those who do.

(6) Good humor. Avoid sourness, pettiness, revenges. Admit it when you're wrong, insist serenely and forever when you're right.

(7) Poise. This is allied with good humor. Poise implies strength, means firmness.

"Good writing," Smith declares, "is something that a writing man must cultivate with his own hands and brain. Expertness in writing comes only with experience in writing. It is gained with much diligence and hard work."

Five Rules

In a speech entitled "It's the Way It's Written," Smith offers five rules for good writing:

(1) You have to care about it tremendously. ("Get by. Do just enough. Put over a good bluff. Don't kill yourself"—you'll hear it—the great American invitation to mediocrity.)

(2) Work like the devil. You won't burn yourself up. You get hardened like steel. Your literary style becomes like steel, too—a sharp and unbreakable weapon in your hand.

How do reporters work so hard? They're not supermen—they just work as if they were.

(3) Write, write your heads off. Write all the time, whether you feel like it or not.

Nobody is going to make a writer of you. Writers are self-made.

(4) Hang around writers. Strive for simplicity, dignity, beautiful reticence.

(5) Read. Read those who give you the feeling "I've struck something new. This fellow makes me see things. This man is strong medicine."

Learn by Mistakes

"Teach yourself by your own mistakes," says William Faulkner, distinguished novelist. "People learn only by error."

Is there a formula one can follow in order to become a good writer?

"Yes," says Faulkner. "It is 99% talent, 99% discipline and 99% work."

One must never be satisfied with what he does, he adds. It is never as good as it can be done. Always dream and shoot higher than you know you can.

"Don't bother to be just better than your contemporaries or your predecessors," he says. "Try to be better than yourself."

Concerning Style

In a recent creative writing class at Columbia University, the instructor asked if there were any questions.

"Yes," replied one young man, "I have two. First, what kind of pen name is most successful? Second, what kind of style should I decide to adopt?"

The sad thing about this is that too many young writers suffer the same lack of understanding about success in writing.

They continually dream of finding Quickie Success Gimmicks.

"As to the pen name, one merely pleases oneself," the instructor said. "It is the writing that succeeds, not the name."

She paused, as if gathering her forces. "As to style, you don't decide to adopt it. You *become* it. Your style is *you* showing through your words."

In his book *The Importance of Living,* Lin Yutang says this:

"Style is not a method, a system, or even a decoration for one's writing.

"It is but the total impression that the reader gets of the quality of the writer's mind, his depth or superficiality, his insight or lack of insight and other qualities like wit, humor, biting sarcasm, genial understanding, kindly cynicism or cynical kindness, hardheadedness, practical common sense and general attitude toward things."

Chapter XXII

A DO-IT-YOURSELF PROGRAM

What can you do specifically to help yourself improve your writing?

This chapter is a special kind of summary, designed to offer you definite answers to that question, to suggest certain procedures so you can turn your good intentions into action.

(1) Always keep in mind this basic idea: *Have something to say and try to say it well.*

You must know what you want to convey to the reader. Many times this should be written as a complete statement. For busy work? No, just to make sure that *you* know exactly what ideas you want to express.

Remember: The reader is never going to have any better understanding of your idea than you do. If you are hazy about this, he will be hazy.

Sometimes it is sufficient to make notes only. The point is, you must be very sure of yourself here. Otherwise, much, if not all, of your additional effort is lost.

(2) Read widely that which is of worth, that which will help you set standards for yourself.

"You have to read the work of masters in order to know what the standard of excellence is," says Katherine Anne Porter, distinguished novelist.

"In recent years students have the idea that you don't have to *read* in order to *write*. In very large colleges where I've gone as guest writer or lecturer, they have had enormous classes of young people who were going to learn to write—and it turned out that they had never read—really read—a good book."

(3) Study models to see how others who write effectively get their ideas into words.

(4) Work at making yourself a more interesting person.

Cultivate many interests, broaden your background. Learn to make friends easily so you can understand people.

Study people—what they do, what they say, why they feel as they do, what they want, what makes them tick.

(5) Develop a "listening ear" for language. Read aloud all you possibly can, from a great variety of authors.

Revising your story means long sessions at your typewriter or with a pencil. This requires the kind of concentration that serves as mental earplugs when you are chumily surrounded by laughing people and clicking typewriters.

Try reading Francis Bacon's "Of Studies." It is a delightful way to gain an understanding of correct compounding of ideas and use of parallelism.

(6) Write fully, volubly—and then condense.

Brevity is an essential ingredient of good writing, says Charles Ferguson, of the *Reader's Digest*. Stressing this to a group of writers at a writers' conference, he pointed out that *brevity is not briefness, nor shortness.*

"Brevity," he said, "is a result of having written out fully, or outlining in detail, and then having carefully selected. It is achieved only by a stern editorial process."

"If you would be pungent, be brief," wrote Robert Southey, "for it is with words as with sunbeams—the more they are condensed, the deeper they burn."

(7) Consider your words.

"Careful with fire" is good advice, we know;
"Careful with words" is ten times doubly so.

This little jingle may have more to do with effect than effectiveness—but it's worth remembering for both reasons.

The creative power of words as a magical instrument in the hands of the writer is described thus by Wilfred Peterson in *The Art of Getting Along*:

"Soft words sung in a lullaby will put a babe to sleep. Exalted words will stir a mob to violence. Eloquent words will send armies marching into the face of death.

"Encouraging words will fan to flame the genius of a Rembrandt or a Lincoln.

"Powerful words will mold the public mind as the sculptor molds his clay.

"Our words are immortal. They go marching through the years in the lives of all those with whom we come in contact."

(8) Learn all you can about the use of language.

Diligently enlarge your vocabulary so you have a feeling for the right word in the right place.

In this age of over-simplification, the language naturally becomes a target for improvement—but all writers must be mindful that *ideas are not being over-simplified*.

Since the purpose of language is to communicate ideas, it would be much better for writers to avoid any kind of "simplifying" that restricts complete expression of meaning.

(Mrs. Albert Einstein was asked one day if she understood her husband's theories.

"Well," she replied, "I understand the words, but I don't always understand the sentences.")

(9) Strive for good English.

What is good English? you ask.

"Good English is the English that is most effective in a particular time and place," says Bergen Evans in *Comfortable Words*, "the English that says most precisely just what we want to say, with the proper emotional overtones and with grace and force and beauty."

(10) Work for simplicity, clarity, color.

To repeat: "Clearness plus color equals copy that clicks."

Practice these aids in expression:

(a) Think in technicolor.

(b) Learn how to "talk in pictures."

(c) Dramatize the action.

(d) Go over your copy painstakingly to see if you have misleading or ambiguous phrases. Even the best organization of ideas will fail if the wording is careless.

For example, note the following sentences, heard on the same newscast:

(1) Jones strove with Barton an hour to capture the runaway boat. (Does this mean that Jones was alongside Barton, or opposing him?)

(2) By 1970 soybean producers may grow soybeans without price support. (Does this mean it will be possible, or does it imply permission?)

Old advice but still good: "Say all you have to say in the fewest possible words, or your reader will skip them," says John

Ruskin, "and in the plainest possible words, or he will certainly misunderstand them."

(11) Constantly remind yourself that writing must be selective.

You cannot include everything that goes into the making of any one story. Learn to select key points, the best illustration, the most suitable quotes, the words that will say the most in the least space.

Consider: The photographer does not take a picture of "just anything" that comes before his camera.

An experienced photographer takes pains to set up the picture so it will tell the viewer what he wants it to say. An artistic photographer exercises even more selectivity in creating the picture he visualizes, so that it will be an expression of the idea as he imagines it.

Caution for writers: The selectivity, the editing must not distort the experience.

About selectivity in movie-making this example: It was said that some 30 hours of photography went into the making of the film produced for the Newspaper Fund, Inc., "Did You Hear What I Said?"—and yet the finished product runs about 30 minutes.

(12) Cultivate enthusiasm so your copy will be lively.

"Much of what we read *lacks giddyap*," says Charles Ferguson, of the *Reader's Digest*.

Another way of saying this is voiced by Lester Markel, of the *New York Times:* "We are, as it were, the Frank Bucks of journalism; we go out to bring back articles—alive, we hope, but too often not."

(13) Let yourself be original.

Trust yourself, from your very first story. Study your subject, decide how you think it would be effectively presented, and then throw all your powers into trying to make it work out in words as you imagine it.

Originality is not being spectacularly different—it is not creating "odditiques."

"The most original authors are not so because they advance what is new," said Goethe many years ago, "but because they put what they have to say as if it had never been said before."

Concerning creative imagination, Sir Joshua Reynolds stressed the point that what we create is actually a new combination of the various images that we have previously gathered and deposited in our experience.

"Nothing can be made up of nothing," he said. "He who has laid up no materials can produce no combinations."

By thoughtful reading, the beginning writer will discover that in writing, even in news reporting, form should be subordinate to function.

The story should be told in whatever form the writer considers best suited to transfer the meaning from his mind to the reader's mind.

Originality, we would emphasize, consists in *thinking for yourself,* not merely in thinking *unlike* other people.

By Way of Summary

The qualities of good journalistic writing are well summed up in the tribute paid by *Dateline* to Laura Bergquist, of *Look,* upon her winning an Overseas Press Club Award:

"Her work is in the best tradition of the craft—combining background knowledge, effective first-person investigation and highly readable prose."

Chapter XXIII

REVISE, REVISE, REVISE

"Often writing is nine-tenths rewriting." This is a note which you should letter carefully and tape to your typewriter.

Beginning journalists are apt to think that successful writers, whether young or not so young, know some magic formula that goes into effect the minute they sit down at a typewriter, helping them produce reams of good copy as fast as they can touch the keys.

Dreaming fondly of the day when they can do likewise, many beginners expect to achieve this magic touch by one hasty draft after another.

This is not the way to writing success.

Teacher's Aid

The student journalist is fortunate in having a teacher who will point out his shortcomings and indicate what can be done by way of improvement.

One can, of course, do this for himself, but the process is slow and shadowy with discouragement.

With guidance one does not have to discover where his story is weak but only how to revise it for greater effectiveness.

In stressing this effort needed for revision, Charles Ferguson, of the *Reader's Digest,* had this to say at a writers conference:

"Seeing improvement in our copy as we revise helps to sustain us in any drudgery that the process of revision involves.

"Indeed, drudgery is not the right word even for the most laborious and exacting phases of writing.

"Revision, properly undertaken, can be as imaginative and satisfying as the original creation.

"Improvement from draft to draft is the dearest reward of the writer. And even if the draft he starts with is lousy, he still has a chance to apply all he knows to the task of licking his cub into shape. There is always an element of hope left, no matter how poor the original copy."

Meaning of Revision

At this point, let's stop for two important questions:

(1) Do you really understand what we mean by revising your story?

(2) Do you know what to do in order to revise your story?

Many students think revision simply means copying the story —same mistakes, same inadequacies.

Finding exactly the right word may mean special effort. But when you know precisely what you want to say, you want precise words to use.

Others think it means checking spelling and being sure the commas are in the right places.

Explanation:

Revision means reworking your story so it is more effective.

This reworking has to do with such fundamentals as

(1) reorganizing of ideas,

(2) rephrasing of sentences,

(3) substituting more adequate words,

(4) including more specific examples,

(5) revamping the lead, possibly starting off on an entirely new idea,

(6) reshaping the entire story,

(7) going forth in search of additional information to round out sections that are not complete.

Checklist for Revision

This list of specific points to check will help you develop an understanding about revision—if you use them.

To use them means that you go over each story you write question by question. You ask yourself the question, you listen to the answer you give yourself, and then you *do something about it.*

You repeat this process until you are satisfied or until you run out of time.

(1) Does the lead seem adequate? Do you feel that the story follows naturally from this lead?

(2) Can you trace your line of thought from the lead to the conclusion?

(3) Do the various parts of the story seem to stand in proper relationship to one another and to be in proportion?

(4) Read your story aloud. Does it "sound right"? Cadence and rhythm are qualities that you will develop by cultivating a "listening ear."

(5) Consider your verbs. Study each sentence with the purpose of finding the strongest verbs suitable for the phrasing of your idea.

For example, did he laugh, or chortle? Did he putter, or piddle? Did the team defeat their opponents, or edge them out? Did he state this, or announce it, or declare it?

(6) Are allusions, illustrations and the like well chosen?

(7) Check all important words to see that you have the exact word in the right place.

(8) Study your sentence structure. Avoid stringy sentences —that is, those with adjective clauses and other kinds of floating modifiers carelessly tacked on at the end. Learn to distinguish between loose and periodic sentences—and then use them as you think they are suited to your purpose.

Avoid long modifiers sandwiched between the essentials of the sentence.

(9) Check for misplaced modifiers, ambiguity, dangling constructions.

(10) Have you dramatized your story where possible?

(11) Have you appealed to the reader's senses as fully as seems suitable for this story? That is, have you given him something to see, to hear, to feel, to smell, to taste?

(12) Note your transitions and connectives to be sure that they are correctly chosen and that you do not repeat noticeably.

(13) Scan the opening words of the paragraphs to be sure that you do not begin paragraphs too much alike.

(14) Consider what you have learned about the devices of rhetoric to see if any apply here.

(15) Check for parallelism, climax, contrast, figures of speech, and the like. Is the phrasing correct?

Each Story Unique

The importance of careful work on each story is emphasized by J. Edward Murray, of the *Arizona Republic*.

"Each story is different," he says. "Therefore, each complex job of organizing, lightening, brightening, correcting and headlining a specific piece of copy, under the circumstances and the time available, must be unique.

"What you don't see—what the reader doesn't see—that is,

that which was eliminated or added, or amended—is as important as what the reader finally sees in print."

Encouraging Word

Does this amount of effort put in on revision seem overwhelming?

Remember: When you become a writer, even a very young, beginning writer, you are in the company of some of the world's greatest figures.

Let the knowledge that they labor over their work inspire and encourage you. Tolstoy, it is said, rewrote most of the twelve hundred pages of *War and Peace* seven times. Edna St. Vincent Millay admits that she has held poems many months, feeling that she might perfect lines with which she was not satisfied.

Caring is what counts.

PART SIX

A Word from the Professional Journalist

Success in interviewing, we have said, comes from doing.

From doing two things: (1) making a determined effort to conduct an interview to the best of our ability in the light of our understanding, and (2) studying the techniques that professional writers say have served them well.

Some of the nation's most successful writers share their ideas with beginning journalists in the following open letters:

Key Word Is "Know"
Be sure that you know the subject which you wish to discuss. Be sure that you know the area of interest of the individual whom you are interviewing.

Know the subject well enough to be able to ask intelligent and penetrating questions.

Know it well enough that if the interviewee says something significant, you appreciate this fact.

If you follow the rules of the above paragraphs, you will have no difficulty, regardless of whom you are talking to, or the subject of the conversation.—Harrison E. Salisbury, assistant managing editor, *New York Times.*

Prepare Intelligently
The most vital thing an interviewer can do is to inform himself intelligently on the subjects about which he hopes to question the interviewee.

Callow and ignorant interviewers do themselves and their task great harm. It is of course impossible for the interviewer to make himself really authoritative on the subjects about which he

Asking questions about a subject you don't understand is important if you want your readers to understand. After the interview, you may need to visit the interviewee for clarification—even if it means seeking the physics teacher at speech tryouts. But bolster your courage—keep asking.

is asking questions, but he can be intelligent and well informed on these subjects.

If he shows the interviewee that he has himself made careful preparation, his prospects for getting satisfying answers will be greatly increased.—Erwin D. Canham, editor in chief, *Christian Science Monitor*.

Four Problems

Interviewing is very important, and young journalists do have problems with it.

Chief among these problems is the failure to find out anything. This is often the result of timidity. The young reporter may hesitate to ask questions about points that he doesn't understand, for fear of revealing his ignorance.

If the subject mentions the Smith Act, and the reporter has never heard of it, the reporter should say, "I'm sorry, Senator, but I'm not familiar with the Smith Act. How does that affect this proposal?"

He should ask questions about everything he doesn't understand, even if he has to run on at boring length. Experienced reporters are never bashful about revealing the gaps in their knowledge, which are considerable and are taken for granted by most interviewees.

Sometimes, however, the reporter's problem is not timidity but ignorance. He may be very outgoing but not smart enough to ask the necessary questions. Such reporters should be advised to enter another line of work.

I have noticed a third kind of difficulty. A young reporter may be both confident and smart, but may be prone to try to impress interviewees with his knowledge of their field. This kind of reporter often will come back with nothing but the memory of a pleasant chat.

The solution here, of course, is for the reporter to ask good questions instead of impressive ones, and to listen more.

Finally, young reporters have difficulty giving a good account of what they have found out.

154   A Word from the Professional Journalist

They must learn to write, by practicing and by studying good writing.—Murray M. Weiss, managing editor, *New York Herald Tribune.*

Carefulness Counts

Careful preparation is the key to successful interviewing.

The journalist should know something about the person to be interviewed as well as the subject matter to be discussed, even if this knowledge does not go beyond a quick glance at the library files.

Beyond this, the reporter will want to keep in mind the pervasive question of *why*—Why am I doing this interview?

In answering the *why,* the reporter begins to build his story. And, as the interview develops, he usually spots the lead for his story as it comes along. With any luck at all, the skeleton of the story builds in the back of the reporter's mind as the questions and answers continue. When the skeleton is finished, so is the interview.

Interviews with students—as for "Personality of the Month"—become more than trite recitals of preferences when you can get the interviewees to talking about their special interests. This interviewee happened to be sketching designs for the yearbook cover when the reporter arrived. Being prepared, she could ask pertinent questions that merited meaningful answers.

Most reporters on general assignment come to interviews with only limited background, sometimes not even including the quick look at the library files. That is why it is essential never to end an interview without asking the subject if he is satisfied that you have covered all the territory.

"Well, that covers the questions I had in mind, but do you think we have left anything out?" the reporter might say.

Or, another useful approach is to say:

"If you were writing this story, what would you regard as the most important thing to tell the readers?"

Both of these questions help the subject to communicate. And, after all, a reporter is merely an agent to get the subject's ideas to the readers.

The more distinguished the subject, the more preparation there should be. There is nothing more insulting to a world figure than to ask him how to spell his name or where he was born when any reporter worth his salt would know that biographical references or the newspaper file have all those answers.

There is another reason for careful preparation. If the reporter shows some knowledge of the elementary aspects of a subject, he will guide the subject past platitudes and into discussion of greater importance.

One British reporter that I know has developed a special style in dealing with diplomats, assuming a posture of knowing all sorts of secrets to the extent that the ego of the diplomats often drives them to demonstrate that they know even more than the reporter and to share all sorts of inside information. The fact that this particular reporter is a woman may have something to do with it, of course.

Preparation also can include drafting questions ahead of time as reserve ammunition in case you blank out on new ideas. When I have participated in television network news interview programs, I have always tried to have a score of useful questions, because that is no time to be caught speechless.

But the best questions, and the newsiest, usually develop spontaneously as the result of careful probing, making the subject justify his answers, letting no careless answers slip by.—Louis B. Fleming, United Nations correspondent, *Los Angeles Times.*

Learn by Practice

I think the best way to learn interviewing is by practice.

There is nothing like the give and take between a well-informed subject and a well-informed interviewer who has questions at his fingertips.

People being interviewed do not want to use up too much of their precious time. Therefore a person doing such a piece of journalism should quickly establish friendly rapport, then go into the interview with well-phrased and effective questions . . .

In writing a news story or feature, one must make a continuing effort to keep it interesting and appealing. This can become second-nature after awhile. But at the start, one must ask one's self, as the paragraphs roll out of the typewriter:

Am I saying things that will hold the reader's attention? Or am I lapsing into dullness, laboring overmuch, smothering my thought with unnecessary words, losing my continuity?

Countless devices are available to maintain interest: use of unusual or colorful words, narrative style, a sense of deep truth, personal involvement, a feel of excitement.

The business of writing a story is much simpler if one knows his facts thoroughly. Then the story virtually writes itself. It's when one doesn't know the picture he is trying to portray, that writing becomes arduous and complicated.—William H. Stringer, chief of London Bureau, *Christian Science Monitor.*

Flexibility Necessary

Perhaps the most important aspect of interviewing a news source comes in the preparation for that interview.

A good reporter will attempt to find out everything he can about the individual he is to interview. If the man happens to be an official of a company, he will also try to learn in advance all he can about the company.

To illustrate, I know of one instance where a *Wall Street*

The beginning writer should start his string book with his first story. Clip carefully, paste neatly, identify with name of publication and date.

Journal reporter was trying to get a very difficult source to admit he had made an investment in a particular project.

In doing his homework in advance of the interview, he ran across an unconfirmed report that the man had invested $77,000 in a project.

In the interview he asked the man, "How did you happen to invest $77,000 in the XYZ project?"

The figure happened to be accurate, and the man being interviewed assumed the reporter knew a good deal more than he did about the investment. Consequently, he offered an explanation as to why he had made the investment.

If the reporter had simply asked, "Did you invest in the XYZ project?" the chances are overwhelming that the man would have denied making the investment.

As part of my preparation for an interview, I write down a list of questions I intend to ask.

Naturally I try to start with the friendliest and easiest questions and save for the last those that the source may be more reluctant to answer.

One thing, however, is important in an interview—flexibility.

It is impossible to chart in advance exactly how an interview will go. Sometimes your source will make a comment that suggests a whole new avenue to explore.

The good reporter will promptly abandon—for the time being —his planned list of questions and go down that unexplored avenue.

I think there is one common danger that all of us are subject to, but especially the new reporter.

It is the tendency to adopt the point of view of the man being interviewed. It is natural to be sympathetic with a fellow human being. However, it is easy to over-indulge this instinct.

If you are not careful, you may find the man you are questioning guiding the interview to subjects which he finds especially interesting or he thinks are important.

I am not advocating an unfriendly attitude at all, but I am

suggesting that it takes a kind of mental toughness to make a good reporter.—Ed Cony, managing editor, *Wall Street Journal.*

Winning Confidence

Interviewing is the heart of news work.

A reporter can and should read other publications for the background of problems, and he should consult his publication's file of old clippings on the matter at issue, but he must always get what is "new"—today's development in the story—by asking experts for information on what has happened since the time of his file.

The reporter must win the confidence of the person he interviews. He must put him at ease by giving him to believe that he is being understood, that he will not be embarrassed by misquotations, and that he will be treated fairly.

Sometimes the news source will speak only on a "not for attribution basis," meaning "don't say who told you." That is O.K. if you can be sure that he is honest and informed. Otherwise you may be holding the bag on a lie or on a deceptive trial balloon.

Roscoe Drummond, the columnist, tells me that his technique is to trade information.

He always brings a tidbit of late news which the congressman of the moment has not heard and is glad to know. That is easier than you think. None of us have time enough to keep up with all the things we want to know, so all of us can bring "news" to the next one.

Roscoe says that after a while his sources feel that he is so valuable a news source for them that they can't afford not to grant a requested interview.

That way Roscoe gets busy men to give him the occasional half hour he needs. Getting people to block out time for you on their crowded calendars is a problem.

Stewart Alsop, an editor of the *Saturday Evening Post,* goes to talk to the man lowest down the organizational scale who still knows the story. Maybe in an embassy everyone from the ambassador on down to the second secretary has the facts on something.

Stew sees the second secretary who is flattered at the attention and speaks more freely than those above. The others may realize the explosive consequences of publication of the news and may not talk to a newsman. That way Stew gets stories which others may be wrongfully covering up.

I was in Moscow for three months in 1958. I asked for interviews with the fifteen top personalities and ended up with an interview with the head of the Orthodox Church in Moscow (an interesting talk about religion under Communism) and with cocktail party encounters with Khrushchev and the one woman in the fifteen-person committee running Russian Communism —Madame Furtseva.

The technique here was: ask for them all and do the best you can with whoever you get.

Prepare for an interview beforehand. Learn all you can about a man and the subject.

Sometimes a prominent man will talk as long as you wish, and you can't use that without a prepared list of topics.

When Nasser seized the Suez Canal in 1956, he gave me the first interview to an American reporter after that rather piratical act.

We talked 90 minutes until I broke it up and in that time discussed everything but Israel ("I don't want to mix in that problem with the one I have").

Be sure you quote a man accurately and fairly. Don't make him sorry he received you.—Barrett McGurn, foreign correspondent, *New York Herald Tribune*.

For Girls Only

"Journalism has been growing more complicated every day," declared Dorothy Kilgallen, late of the *New York Journal American,* in recalling some of her experiences while covering the wedding of Princess Grace of Monaco.

"I had eleven pieces of luggage . . . but there's just no way of covering a royal wedding without the proper equipment . . . a sapphire mink stole . . . an ermine wrap . . . a little chinchilla wrap . . . a white cashmere coat . . . a gold brocade evening coat."

A different look at the subject is voiced by Sally Gibson, an advertising executive, in a speech entitled "It's a Man's World—Enjoy It."

"I do not call myself a career woman," she says. "I am a woman. It is because I am a woman that I *have* the career. You are employed *because* you are a woman.

"If they wanted a man on the job, they would hire one.

"Don't slip out of your high heels and clobber around in brogues too big and too tough for you to fill. Stay in your I. Miller's, girls. Be sure they're pretty and *be sure you fill them well* —and you'll do better than you ever dreamed."

PART SEVEN

Suggestions from Student Editors

Editors of high school publications frequently are able to make suggestions and offer advice about helpful techniques in areas where the beginner will be doing his first work.

Obviously, a beginner will work on the school scene. His assignments will concern students, his stories will be evaluated by student editors, and his reading public will be the student body.

Consequently, though he has studied the methods and listened to the advice of professional journalists, his immediate efforts will be on a student level.

Because of this, he will be best able to judge what is expected of him if he can use student work as guides.

The following pages include a number of suggestions framed by students and examples written by students so the beginner can have some standard of comparison.

Most of these were worked out in a workshop where the task at hand was to compile a series of stories to serve as guides and to accompany the body of rules and suggestions to which a beginner must necessarily be introduced.

Personality Interview
  (1) Ineffective way to do the story:

GIRL OF THE MONTH

Chosen as this week's senior of the week, Jo Burton is an outstanding example of all-round talent.

Her statistics include: height five feet six inches, hazel colored eyes and a friendly smile.

She lists her favorite food as hamburgers and French fries, her favorite colors are light blue and green, her favorite song is "Paint It Black" by the Rolling Stones, and her all-time favorite movie is "Inside Daisy Clover."

Jo says that she has really enjoyed her three years here in high school. She was elected president of the local Red Cross chapter, where she teaches swimming lessons to retarded children. A real worker—that's Jo.

(This piece shows very little effort on the part of the writer. Obviously, a questionnaire was handed to the subject. Probably the answers were given in paragraph form just as they came in order on the questionnaire. The writer overlooked the most interesting and different feature mentioned, the swimming lessons. Note the editorialized space-filler for the ending.)

(2) Better:

GIRL SWIMMING INSTRUCTOR
HELPS HANDICAPPED CHILDREN

Usually the scene of light-hearted fun, the Girls Club swimming pool becomes a classroom with a definite purpose on Monday nights when students from the Joseph M. Hill School for the Handicapped come to the Club for swimming lessons.

The warm, clear water is soothing and the voice of the instructor is encouraging: "Pretend you're in the bathtub, relax . . . pretend you've dropped the soap . . . now reach down . . . pick it up . . ."

Jo Ellen Burton, THS senior, is an instructor in the Red Cross program that furnishes swimming lessons to mentally and physically handicapped children.

"Teaching the children serves a two-fold purpose," she said. Primarily the lessons help them learn to follow instructions, but we also teach them water safety."

Jo's hazel eyes danced as she glanced around the pool, waiting for the children to come in.

Selected Bits of Free Advice

. . . gleaned from the pros and learned by experience

You've decided whom you want to interview. You've made your appointment and arrived on time. Your next objective is to establish rapport with your subject as quickly as possible.

* * *

The approach that works best for me is to lead the person to talk about what he does. I've found that asking someone to talk about himself makes some people a bit shy, but most people warm quickly to talking about their jobs, hobbies, or pet causes.

* * *

Keep in mind that many people will be concerned about how they appear in print. Unless your subject is relaxed and unguarded, he will not be as spontaneous as you want him to be.

* * *

Prepare questions before you go and read background information if possible. This shows the interviewee that you care enough to bother. However, if you are totally unaware of your subject, ask your interviewee for background.

* * *

Look at your subject's surroundings. Look at your subject. What are his mannerisms, how does he dress? What kind of things—books, objects, furnishings—reflect his tastes and circumstances?

* * *

Shy or outgoing, most people really do like to talk about themselves.

Becky Meeks, woman's page editor,
Southwest Times Record

"It's exciting," she smiled, "just to see how much they learn to help themselves, even in one evening."

Is this kind of teaching hard?

She pondered the question thoughtfully. "No, just requires a lot of patience, mostly."

A great deal of repetition is necessary, she added.

"Even getting them to put their faces under the water is a great accomplishment," she said. "It makes all my work worth the effort, because handicapped children especially fear the water."

She stretched a little, as if to relax all her muscles.

"Another thing," she observed, "is that you have to keep in excellent physical condition and be strong. I practice about five hours a week preparing for these lessons."

Trim in a blue-green ruffled swimsuit as she stretched to her full length, about five six, she looked like anything but a typical "lady gymster." Her short brown hair fluffed up in bouncy little curls.

"This work has greatly influenced my life," she said seriously. "I want to continue doing this kind of thing."

Planning to major in special education in college, she hopes now to become an instructor for retarded children in music therapy.

(This shows a better way to tell a story about Jo. It is not a perfect story, as those that follow are not perfect—but it shows how to seek out unusual interests and write about those.)

Academic Subjects

SIMPLICITY OF CHILD'S WORLD REFLECTED IN HIS ART

Simplicity is the word for children's art.

Thus Sister Roberta, art instructor at Saint Scholastica Academy, summarized the annual Young Arkansas Artists Show held this month at the Fine Arts Center in Little Rock.

"Children's art is simple because their world is simple," Sister Roberta explained.

This simplicity is visible in the economy of line and form that the children display in their work.

"Children's art is also very primitive," she said. "These children are not bothered by the inhibitions that adult art displays. They are not afraid of being different. Until a child becomes aware of the outside world, he paints only what he knows, as he knows it."

Although children display a total disregard for adult concepts, they show a natural employment of aesthetic devices, she pointed out.

"They produce fresh color schemes and spatial designs out of instinct," she added.

A child follows no formula for putting together pictorial elements. It is therefore a spontaneous form of art.

"Recognition of the importance of natural freeness accompanied by simplicity are the most valuable lessons to be learned from the art displayed here," said Sister Roberta.

The question of society's influence on children's art is dramatically shown in a comparison of the drawings of Hawaiian children, also included in the show, with those done by the young Arkansas artists.

Even though the paintings are done by children the same age, there is a marked difference in subject matter, color and style.

"As soon as a child becomes aware of the world around him, his art begins to become more 'schooled,' " she explained. "Naturally, different cultures cause art to take divergent paths. A child is influenced by all that is around him—television, comics, cartoons, other children's work and his own observations."

Another example of the influence of outside sources is shown when the child ceases to use the marginal line in his art. This, she pointed out, is the heavy line that forms the base of most young children's drawings.

It is drawn straight across the page and all objects sit directly on it. The sky is a blue swab across the top of the page and usually does not meet the ground.

"As a child observes nature and society's interpretation of it with a keener eye, he realizes that this line is incorrect and changes his style to suit his new standards," she said. "In this way the child's art has been modified by the world around him."

From the 1,026 pieces submitted by 92 schools, a jury of university art instructors selected the 250 now being shown.

"I would find it very hard to judge a show of this nature," Sister Roberta said. "Each child's art is original and personal, and no set of rules exists by which to grade a child's picture. There can be no best picture—all are valuable."

(This story shows correct use of quotes and summary.)

General Subject

(The following story shows how a school paper can handle a story on some subject about which the students should be informed.)

TRADITIONAL REPORTING SYSTEM
SURVIVES IN SPITE OF FAULTS

Are report cards here to stay?

Recent experiments in various schools throughout the country involving the abolition of report cards provide a sound basis for such a question.

Ralph Ramsey, assistant superintendent of the Bonneville schools, answers this question for the local district—yes.

"Report cards will generally remain in use, for they have become a tradition in the American schools, both public and private," he stated. "It is probable that they will remain the chief communication between teacher, student and parent. We plan to continue the use of report cards here."

Any deviation from this system usually meets with resistance from educators, school patrons, parents and the public in general.

"Just as traditional as the report card is the letter grade system of symbol used to denote pupil achievement in a given subject," he added. "This system has been questioned but still seems to be sound."

Some deviations from the letter grade have been mildly successful, including the number system and the percentage system.

"This grading system has obvious weaknesses," he pointed out. "Chief among these is brevity. Very little vital information can be placed on a report card to tell the pupil or parent the complete story of pupil progress."

In many schools teachers have attempted to overcome this weakness by following up report cards with parental conferences.

"Another weakness of the report card lies in the fact that no matter what system of symbols is used to report achievement, each teacher considers different factors or weights to grade pupils," he said.

Thus, he added, every mark is a matter of individual interpretation.

"In like manner, the pupil and parent interpret, or misinterpret, as the case may be, the information on the card," he commented.

Therefore, even the most objective set of symbols become subjective when interpreted by different teachers or schools evaluating them.

"However, some method of reporting and evaluating is necessary," he said. "While the report card does have many weaknesses, it can and does perform these necessary functions."

Interesting Visitor

TV'S "WISHBONE" VISITS
LOCAL RODEO

"I was born in New Mexico in 'muleskinner country' but when I became a regular on the 'Rawhide' video series, I had to have a 'secret' driver handle the team of horses."

These are the words of Paul Brinegar, "Wishbone" on a TV

Western that has the sought after secret of longevity on the "vast wasteland."

He is appearing here this week in connection with the annual livestock exposition and rodeo.

"The first time I got up on that wagon, the horses almost ran away with me," the supposedly experienced Westerner said in a press conference here today. "The producers put a stunt man underneath the wagon box to handle the reins. Televiewers, however, thought I was doing the driving."

Despite these early problems, the doughty Brinegar has become a beloved television favorite. In recent weeks he has literally taken the reins, which he once could not handle, of the hour-long program.

While Eric Fleming and Clint Eastwood are in the midst of a cast shake up, Brinegar is riding high—and safe. He just signed another long-term contract.

"In one program, viewers saw me literally beaten to a pulp," he laughed. "Actually, the man who was taking the beating (from a gang of desperate outlaws) was my stunt man again. As a matter of fact, he's my exact double."

His gray eyes danced. "Don't worry. I'm me."

Brinegar had advice for Hollywood hopefuls.

"Working in Hollywood was what I'd wanted all my life, so I guess I'm lucky," he said seriously. "But there are thousands who will never make it, already there, now. Too many people who have talent can't find a job."

(In this story the reader would be interested in knowing how he looked, what he was wearing, what kind of person he is "off-stage.")

Interesting Situation

SUPERINTENDENT MUST SOLVE
WEATHER PROBLEMS, TOO

"One of the toughest decisions that I make is 'Should we or should we not close the schools for snow?'" stated Dr. Carl

Hansen, superintendent of D.C. public schools, at an interview February 9 at Franklin School.

"If the District and Federal employees are let off, we are dismissed," he continued. "However, we have the authority to close the schools if the situation has special elements which make traveling to school hazardous for children."

In deciding whether to conduct "business as usual," the basic concern is for the safety of the children.

One of the problems in the January storm was the condition of the walks, the superintendent said. Forced to "take to the streets," school children created additional traffic hazards, both for themselves and oncoming traffic.

Although safety is of paramount concern, other factors are considered.

"So many children in our system don't have galoshes," he said. "They just can't come to school when the snow is particularly heavy."

Heavy snow warnings signal full-time operation for the Central Control Station, headed by the Highway Department. A special telephone number yields a direct line to this bureau which issues continuous information on road conditions.

After consulting all reports, Dr. Hansen makes a recommendation to Wesley S. Williams, president of the Board of Education.

"In actuality it is the president of the Board who makes the final decision," Dr. Hansen said.

Central Radio Control issues the Board's verdict to all area radio and television stations. Although the news is generally released before 6 A.M., there are those who can't wait for the official announcement.

"My telephone starts ringing at 12 or 1 A.M.," stated the superintendent.

Composed of parents, teachers and school children, the callers usually want to ask him his decision or to give him advice. During the last storm, a six-year-old child phoned to ask him "not to make us go to school" the next day.

"We have an extra week over the 180 required days against which we can draw," stated Dr. Hansen. (The *Beacon*, Washington, D.C.)

Emphasizing Special Aspect

(The following stories were selected from the *Redbird*, Loudonville, Ohio, to illustrate how a reporter selects from many notes only those items which pertain to a certain aspect. The *Redbird*, a mimeographed paper, makes excellent use of small space. This lack of space is a special problem for mimeographed papers. Often only a skeleton of a story can be run—but the having to write for minimum space is good training.)

EDITOR TRAVELS WIDELY, HAS INTERNATIONAL TASTES

She's any journalist's "dream come true," equipped with international tastes and ideals.

Fitting this description to a "T," Miss Bunny Brower, fashion and travel editor for *Seventeen Magazine*, revealed her transcontinental flare, after addressing the 34th annual JAOS convention.

From the eastern shores of the United States to various countries of Europe—from Montreal to the interior of South America—she has traveled for "personal desires as well as professional."

"I especially like German and Italian operas," she continued, but like the teen-age audience she writes for, she, too, "enjoys the Beatles."

At home the young editor delights in her "big standard, steel gray French poodle" which she affectionately calls Winston.

"Not after the cigarette," she said with a smile, but after the more famous name, Winston Churchill.

One of Miss Brower's most interesting experiences took place when she interviewed Major Titov, the Russian cosmonaut.

"He had a ready smile and good sense of humor, but I feel that much of his personality was lost through the interpreter," she explained.

SANTA CLAUS DISCLOSES SECRETS OF CHRISTMAS CHEER

Santa Claus is living in town.

Although he is just an "average citizen" 11 months of the year, George Bender, longtime Loudonville resident, spends December playing Santa Claus for area youngsters.

From riding in the Christmas parade sponsored by the Retail Merchants Association to visiting private homes on Christmas Eve, the veteran St. Nick has spread joy and Christmas cheer throughout the community for many years.

"By making someone else happy, you become happy yourself," said Mr. Bender, as he explained his "job."

The 59-year-old Santa charges only for appearances in the parade and for giving treats to the children.

Although he masqueraded as the jolly gentleman a few times in earlier years, Loudonville's Santa Claus "retired" from his Christmas occupation because "playing the part of Santa seemed sort of childish."

But when he was approached by the American Legion more recently to hand out candy, Mr. Bender accepted—and since then he has continued his yearly impersonation.

"For the last 15 years I've felt a lot better mentally and physically because of the job," he said with a grin. "The costume and the spirit of giving do something for you."

He is now playing Santa for the sons and daughters of the children he entertained years ago.

Mr. Bender borrowed his first costume, but he has bought two since then. Each good costume, consisting of coat, trousers, cap, boots, wig and whiskers, costs about $80.

However, with special care, a suit will last seven years. The suit may be dry-cleaned, but the nylon hair and beard have to be "washed with very soft soap and waved to perfection by Mrs. Bender," her husband remarked.

Explaining how he makes children happy, Santa Claus Bender said that the big thing is the entrance.

"I try to get the kids excited by making a lot of noise," he laughed. "After ringing some sleigh bells, I usually enter the room with a 'Yo! Ho! Ho!' and then I shake the kids' hands and ask them if they've been good little boys and girls."

Life is not all a bowl of poinsettias for a modern Santa Claus.

Playing Santa involves such problems as getting to the right homes on time Christmas Eve and handling the children.

Recalling his experiences, Mr. Bender told how he often had to divert youngsters from pulling his whiskers.

"You can tell when they're going to do it," he grinned, "because they start watching the beard. When they move, you move. I just hold back their hands and get their attention by talking."

Other problems are the older children who recognize Santa and call him "George."

"Harsh looks in their direction usually quiet them down," he remarked.

"There are also a few youngsters who want to share their candy with me," he continued with a chuckle. "It's hard to refuse, but if I ate candy, I'd have some mighty sticky whiskers."

Although Santa has many years of service under his big black belt, he plans to keep on making the children's Christmas memorable until he "loses his pep."

* * *

Learning the Hard Way

A student editor was addressing beginning reporters at a Minnesota short course:

Learning to ask questions that bring informative answers seems simpler than it is. Beginners can learn some basic helps, but unfortunately, many times one learns the hard way.

Let me tell you what happened to me:

Our staff decided to do a series of special features on teachers. It was my idea—and as a new member of the "features team," I was thrilled to have my proposal accepted.

And I was doubly thrilled when the editor asked me to do the first one, an interview with the new music teacher.

That thrill of excitement—the taste of success—was sweet. My idea accepted, I the chosen one—ahhh—life was good.

I knew all about interviewing, for I had already been on the staff for two weeks! I'd learned the rules: (1) make an appointment, (2) prepare, (3) ask questions.

So I did. (1) I made an appointment for 3:15 the next afternoon, (2) I prepared—with two new pencils and a new notebook, (3) I went to ask questions.

The afternoon was beautiful. The world was mine. At 3:15 I entered the music room.

"Well, hello," he said. "Come in."

For the first time I noticed that he was very young, with dark hair and eyes and a casual, easy manner. The room was orderly, with the music stacked neatly on shelves, except that on a table to one side there were scattered sheets as if someone had been working, and on the table a strange-looking instrument, a musical instrument, I supposed, but new to me.

Me: "I've come to interview you for the paper."

Him: "Yes, thank you."

Me: (Bright and eager to begin) "What is your name?"

Him: (Looking a bit startled) "John Applegate."

Me: "I mean all of your name."

Him: "John William Applegate."

Me: "What is your background?"

Him: "Well, I have a master's degree in music from the state university. I grew up in Faulkner County."

Me: (Now for the Big Question) "What makes you an interesting personality?"

Him: (Shrugging, with a little smile) "Me? An interesting personality?"

Me: "Yes. We are going to run personality features about the new teachers. You're our first one."

Him: "Well—I hardly know—I—well—I—"

Me: "Oh, go ahead. Talk all you want to. That's what makes a good personality feature, lots of information, that is."

Him: "Well—I really—"

Me: "You're enthusiastic about music, aren't you?"

Him: "Yes."

Me: "Well, what are you doing that's interesting?"

Him: "I'm not sure what—"

Me: "Oh, like what's really interesting about you—well, you know—Oh, excuse me, but what is that odd-looking instrument there on the table?"

Him: "Oh, that's a dulcimer."

Me: "A dulcimer? I never heard of one. But back to the interview. I really need to know what makes you an interesting person." (I was about to give up. We weren't getting anywhere.)

Him: "Well—I really never considered myself as—"

Me: "Well, thank you anyway, and I'll just tell the editor I've checked into this."

Him: "Thank you. I'm sorry I couldn't be of more help."

On the way to the J room my spirits sank lower and lower. The interview was a washout. My first assignment was a dud. But he had been nice and friendly, and I liked him anyway. And that strange instrument—what does anybody do with a dulcimer? . . .

Friends, you're probably wondering how anyone could be as dumb as I was about that—but I've discovered that there are others who started out about the same way.

Let me tell you how the editor handled this story:

First, he asked the principal if he might see the background information filled in by new teachers and filed in the office. He learned that Mr. Applegate frequently visited the national folk center at Mountain View, Arkansas (near his home town) and that he not only played the dulcimer but had learned at Mountain View how to make one!

And what is a dulcimer? The editor checked that in the dic-

Suggestions from Student Editors 177

tionary: "a very old musical instrument from which was derived the idea of the piano action, played with two light hammers held in the hands."

Yes, and when he went to see Mr. Applegate, he found that Mr. A. had already asked school permission to organize a group interested in folk study, with a visit to Mountain View a possibility sometime during the fall. . . .

So I learned the hard way. It was bitter at the time to see the editor's story where mine should have—could have—been.

It was a beautiful story—and a good lesson for me. . . .

* * *

Interview in Private

Interviews are always conducted in private, never in a place where the interviewee will be self-conscious because of the presence of his peers.

When I tried to question one student in the journalism office, he hesitated and kept saying, "This is stupid. Nobody will want to read it."

Later when I spoke to him in the relative quiet of a practice room, I got one of the best student interviews I have ever done.

Another help is knowing as much as you can about the person beforehand.

I was interviewing the outstanding actress at HPHS recently. In listing her credits, she failed to mention summer stock work, which I knew she had done.

I mentioned it to her and she replied, "Oh, my gosh, I completely forgot. You know the funniest thing happened there." And she proceeded to tell me how she had ruined her first role (a corpse) by coughing. (*Shoreline,* Highland Park, Illinois)

Exploratory Questions

Generally when we do features concerning teen honorees, there are certain questions that seem appropriate. However, sometimes it is hard to find anything "different" to develop, so we have devised a list of questions that we begin with as sort of "exploratory." They are as follow:

(1) What other schools have you attended? Anything interesting in this connection . . . athletics, student government or club offices, honors, scholastic achievement?
(2) What organizations are you a member of?
(3) What courses are you taking? Interesting projects?
(4) Do you have an out-of-school job?
(5) What kind of schooling or training do you plan to continue after graduation? Career plans?
(6) What are your extracurricular activities?
(7) Do you have a philosophy of life?
(8) What is the funniest incident that has happened to you?
(9) Do you have any pets?
(10) How did you spend last summer?
(11) Have you made any interesting trips? Planning one?
(12) What hobbies and special interests have you?
(13) Have you ever lived in any interesting places?
(14) What sports do you enjoy?
(15) Do you have any pet projects, secret ambitions?
(16) What do you enjoy most about school?
(17) (Get quote from teacher about student.) *Westener World,* Lubbock, Texas)

* * *

Ex-Editor Speaks
Dear Teacher:

When I took this newspaper job last fall, I found myself bewildered and confused, for this was quite different from a high school paper. No longer in school, I couldn't depend on my former sources for story ideas.

These thoughts reminded me of another newspaper, another "first day on the job," for as a sophomore in high school, I had been just as alarmed as this.

For the first two issues, in fact, I did nothing more than write a few fillers. Finally, I approached my editor, a senior, and requested an assignment. She suggested that I do a history-purpose-current activities feature on one of the school organizations.

I wrote out my questions for the club adviser and club president—about twice as many as I thought I would need. And then I went to see them.

When I had written and rewritten the story several times, I turned it in, although I was certain it sounded more like a magazine article than a news feature.

I guess I was about the happiest girl in school when it appeared under a three-column headline. After that, I had more confidence, and therefore the courage to seek out my story ideas.

Two years later, my first couple of weeks as editor of the paper came along. I was as nervous as the proverbial cat.

I decided the theory of writing twice as many questions as I anticipated I needed for a story could apply here too. So I assigned approximately twice as many stories as I thought I would need for the first issue.

It worked!

As the same problem faced me on my "real" job here on the paper—uncertainty and lack of confidence—I thought perhaps I could again get my start from a veteran and gain confidence by planning well.

The sports editor was most helpful, assigning me a color feature on the state university's homecoming game.

I followed the same pattern—*planning ahead* and *preparing plenty of questions*. And I have gained the necessary confidence. (S.S.A.)

* * *

Note Found on the Desk

Maybe somebody can teach somebody to write—but mostly it's a matter of teaching a somebody to be a more interesting somebody.

If you're normally a grumbly-blah person, you're going to write grumbly-blah.

* * *

Next to doing things that deserve to be written, nothing gets a man more credit or gives him more pleasure than to write things that deserve to be read. —Lord Chesterfield

FOR FURTHER READING

Some of the most valuable helps for those who are beginning to work on a high school paper or who are taking up journalism for the first time are the publications offered by the various press associations. These exist at several levels—area, state and national.

By joining these organizations, the staff becomes eligible for a number of free helps. Other publications can be obtained even by non-members. A price list can be obtained upon request.

Many staffs join both their state or area association and one or more of the national groups. Through publications of these national associations, you can locate names of other groups who you think might have publications that would be helpful to you.

NATIONAL ORGANIZATIONS:

Columbia Scholastic Press Association, Box 11, Low Library, Columbia University, New York. Magazine: *School Press Review;* other publications. Director, Charles R. O'Malley.

Columbia Scholastic Press Advisers Association, Box 11, Low Library, Columbia University, New York. Magazine: Bulletin.

National Scholastic Press Association, Suite 205, 720 Washington Avenue S.E., University of Minnesota, Minneapolis, Minnesota. Magazine: *Scholastic Editor—Graphics/Communication;* other publications. "Bookstore Catalog" available.

Quill and Scroll Society, State University of Iowa, Iowa City, Iowa. Magazine: *Quill and Scroll.* Director, Richard Johns.

Future Journalists of America, School of Journalism, University of Oklahoma, Norman, Oklahoma. Director, J. F. Paschal.

SUGGESTED TITLES OF OLDER BOOKS FOR REFERENCE:

Springboard to Journalism, Benjamin Allnutt, 1969, Columbia Scholastic Press Advisers Association, Low Library, Columbia Uni-

For Further Reading

versity, New York. An outline especially helpful to inexperienced advisers.

The Student Journalist, Edmund C. Arnold and Hillier Krieghbaum, 1963, New York University Press, New York. A handbook for adviser and staff. Covers newspaper, yearbook, magazine.

Journalists in Action, Edward Barrett, 1963, Channel Press, Manhasset, Long Island, New York.

The Story of the New York Times, Meyer Berger, 1951, Simon and Schuster, New York.

Watch Your Language, Theodore M. Bernstein, 1958, Channel Press, Great Neck, New York. A guide to correct usage.

Newsmen at Work, Laurence R. Campbell and Roland Wolseley, 1949, Houghton Mifflin, Boston.

Reporting, Mitchell V. Charnley, second edition 1966, Holt, Rinehart and Winston, Inc., New York.

Depth Reporting, An Approach to Journalism, Neale Copple, 1964, Prentice-Hall, Englewood Cliffs, New Jersey. ("A book on the art and science of making news understandable.")

Put It on the Front Page, Please, John Henry Culter, 1960, Ives Washburn, New York.

Ladies, Gentlemen and Editors, Walter Davenport and James C. Derieux, 1960, Doubleday, Garden City, New York.

Post Biographies of Famous Journalists, ed. by John E. Drewry, 1942, University of Georgia Press, Athens, Georgia.

More Post Biographies, ed. by John E. Drewry, 1947, University of Georgia Press, Athens, Georgia.

Scholastic Journalism, Earl English and Clarence Hach, fifth edition, Iowa State University Press, Ames, Iowa.

Say It with Words, Charles Ferguson, 1959, Alfred A. Knopf, New York.

The Art of Plain Talk, Rudolf Flesch, 1946, Harper, New York. One of a number of books by this author, a specialist in writing to be understood.

Get That Story—Journalism, Its Lures and Thrills, John Floherty, 1952, Lippincott, New York. A description of the work and responsibilities of the young reporter.

Keys to Successful Interviewing, Stewart Harral, 1954, University of Oklahoma Press, Norman, Oklahoma.

The Feature Writer's Handbook, Stewart Harral, 1958, University of Oklahoma Press, Norman, Oklahoma.

Foreign Correspondence: The Great Reporters and Their Times, John Hohenberg, 1964, Columbia University Press, New York.

The Professional Journalist, John Hohenberg, 1963, Columbia University Press, New York.

The Pulitzer Prize Story, John Hohenberg, 1965, Columbia University Press, New York.

We Cover the World, ed. by Eugene Lyons, 1937, Harcourt Brace, New York.

Deadlines and Monkeyshines: The Fabled World of Chicago Journalism, John J. McPhaul, 1962, Prentice-Hall, Englewood Cliffs, New Jersey.

American Journalism, Frank Luther Mott, 1941, Macmillan, New York. The most authoritative general history of journalism in the United States.

News Gathering and News Writing, R. M. Neal, 1949, Prentice-Hall, Englewood Cliffs, New Jersey.

The Student Journalist and News Reporting, Hazel Presson, 1966, Richards Rosen Press, New York.

The New World of the Wall Street Journal, ed. by Charles Preston, 1963, Simon and Schuster, New York.

The Newspaper: Its Making and Its Meaning, staff of *The New York Times,* 1945, Charles Scribner's Sons, New York.

Journalism and the School Paper, DeWitt C. Reddick, 1958, Heath, Boston.

Twentieth Century Reporting at Its Best, ed. by Bryce W. Rucker, 1964, Iowa State University Press, Ames, Iowa.

Bury Me in an Old Press Box, Fred Russell, 1957, A. S. Barnes, New York.

Your Future in Journalism, Arville Schaleben, revised edition, 1966, Richards Rosen Press, New York.

Forgive Us Our Press Passes, Elaine Shepard, 1962, Prentice-Hall, Englewood Cliffs, New Jersey.

Masterpieces of War Reporting, ed. by Louis Snyder, 1962, Julian Messner, New York.

A Treasury of Great Reporting, ed. by Louis Snyder and Richard Morris, 1949, Simon and Schuster, New York.

For Further Reading

The Student Journalist and Sports Editing, Harry Stapler, 1964, Richards Rosen Press, New York.

The Student Journalist and Sports Reporting, Harry Stapler, 1964, Richards Rosen Press, New York.

Modern News Reporting, Carl Warren, 1934, Harper, New York.

How to Sell Yourself to Others, Elmer Wheeler, 1947, Prentice-Hall, Englewood Cliffs, New Jersey.

(*Note:* Several of the above books have been, or are being, revised for updating.)

* * *

CONTEMPORARY BIBLIOGRAPHY:

For new titles, as well as for older books now in print, information can be secured from state, regional, and national scholastic press associations. In most instances this information is without charge.

Suggested: ACP/NSPA Bookstore Catalog of Journalism Publications available. Address: ACP/NSPA, Suite 205, 720 Washington Ave. S.E., University of Minnesota, Minneapolis, Minnesota 55414.

* * *

ACKNOWLEDGMENTS

To the many individuals who have contributed in some way to the writing of this book I would like to express a special word of appreciation. Professional journalists, teachers and students, as well as many others who are interested in school publications, have been particularly helpful in the assembling of the material needed.

Among those whom I would like to mention specifically are these:
Paul S. Swensson, Patrick W. Kennedy—the Newspaper Fund, Inc.; Col. Joseph M. Murphy, Charles R. O'Malley—Columbia Scholastic Press Association; Don Carter, the *National Observer;* Clarence O. Schlaver, *Quill;* Lester Benz, Richard Johns—Quill and Scroll Society; C. J. Leabo, National Scholastic Press Association; J. B. Covington, William J. Good—University of Arkansas; William D. Downs, Ouachita Baptist University; Max R. Haddick, Texas Interscholastic League Press Conference; Foster-Harris, C. Joe Holland—University of Oklahoma; J. F. Paschal, Future Journalists of America; Becky Meeks, Jack Moseley—*Southwest Times Record;* Earl Farnsworth, Frank Jones, Linda Rainwater, Tom Oliver—Fort Smith Public School System; Birnie Glennell, Family Enterprises Association; George Hastings.

William H. Stringer, *Christian Science Monitor;* Ed Cony, *The Wall Street Journal;* Louis B. Fleming, *Los Angeles Times;* Murray M. Weiss, *New York Herald-Tribune;* Erwin D. Canham, *Christian Science Monitor;* Harrison Salisbury, *New York Times;* Barrett McGurn, *New York Herald-Tribune;* Charles Ferguson, *Reader's Digest.*

Sue Sonderegger Angel, Kansas City, Missouri; Pat Best, Tahlequah, Oklahoma; Marjorie Robinson, Loudonville, Ohio; Mary Nell Turner, Hope, Arkansas; Lili Gottfried, Washington, D.C.; William J. Pharis, Donna Riley, Carol Lamoreux, Marsha Hayden, Jim Pat Bell, Mary Gayle Penix, Fort Smith, Arkansas; Elaine Baker, Lubbock, Texas; Carol Nissenson, Highland Park, Illinois; David Bordeaux, Peoria, Illinois.

Acknowledgments

Four other groups should be included for special recognition: those whose papers have come to me through exchange or by special request and from whom I have clipped illustrative material; those in the local school system—the board of education, the superintendent and the principal—whose encouragement makes this kind of undertaking possible; students with whom I have been associated in workshops where our common problems are a continuing subject of discussion; and my own students who have contributed in many ways to the work—and because of whom I like teaching young journalists.

Photographs have been provided by the photography departments of Northside and Southside High Schools in Fort Smith, Arkansas, under the direction of Linda Rainwater and Tom Oliver, respectively. Photographers on special assignment were two Southside seniors who have earned special honors for work in high school publications and have been cited by the Arkansas High School Press Association: Greg Griffin, special awards, and Jim Phillips, state photographer of the year.

(*Note:* In some of the illustrative material submitted by persons of prominence, I have chosen to designate their association with that organization or publication with which I thought readers would be most familiar. In some instances they are now in other positions. Three of the publications mentioned are now either merged or discontinued.)